AF334343

Pinikindu

Pinikindu

Maternal Nurture, Paternal Substance

Brenda Johnson Clay

The University of Chicago Press

Chicago and London

BRENDA JOHNSON CLAY received her Ph.D. from
Southern Illinois University and did research
in New Ireland, Papua New Guinea, under a grant
from the National Science Foundation.

The University of Chicago Press, Chicago 60637
The University of Chicago Press, Ltd., London

Library of Congress Cataloging in Publication Data

Clay, Brenda Johnson.
    Pinikindu : maternal nurture, paternal sub-
stance.

    Bibliography: p.
    Includes index.
    1. Mandak (Papua New Guinea people)   I.   Title.
DU740.42.C58   301.29'95   76-8083
ISBN 0-226-10943-7

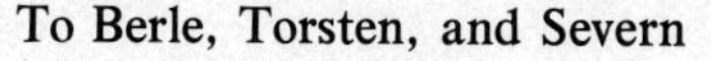

To Berle, Torsten, and Severn

Contents

Illustrations

Foreword

If it has always been something of an anthropological truism that one can find perfectly good subjects for field research anywhere, it is also a limiting condition. Anthropologists working in New Guinea seem often to have been imbued, like the adventurers and pony soldiers of Custer's day, with a desire to be the last frontiersmen. Yet, although certain research inquiries (or certain dispositions of the researcher) may demand The Last 150 Papuans Never to Have Heard an Airplane Engine, or natives so isolated they have not developed self-consciousness, such novelty in itself contributes little to the intrinsic quality of the resulting study. It has always been the specter of comprehensibility in the exotic that has made special demands on the anthropologist. The Mandak people of New Ireland are quite exotic enough for all their century or so of European contact: the discovery of a matrilineal people who trace substance-connection to the father alone is something of an ethnographic event. But novelty of this sort can scarcely account for what is in many respects the best study of a Melanesian kin complex that has yet appeared.

In her introduction Dr. Clay outlines her theoretical position with telling skill, clarity, and good judgment. It remains for me only to remind strangers to this approach that "symbol" is used here in the broad, phenomenological sense of a semiotic operator through which the totality of perception and ideation can be realized, rather than the narrow sense of a "merely symbolic" conceptual world opposed to "reality." The Mandak culture interpreted by Dr. Clay is no more a derivative spinoff of "nature"—an analogue of our "social contract" view of humanity—than her central concept of "nurture" is a matter of pediatrics and calories. Thus her analysis of the Mandak removes itself from the whole complex of attitudes and assumptions implied by the standard (Cartesian) "culture-nature" orientation: it eludes the petty moralism of brittle definitions and overemphasized "prescriptions" as well as the scientistic determinism of "cognition," naturalism, or "politics and economics." In the final analysis *Pinikindu* does not replicate, measure, or delimit the Mandak, but strives only to come to terms with them, to "turn the talk." It is implicit in this analysis that the Mandak are always more various, imaginative, assertive, recalcitrant, and (necessarily, I think) confused than the account of them: and it is because her viewpoint incorporates this fact that Dr. Clay's book is something more than the ordinary anthropological monograph.

Pinikindu does not predicate the Mandak, but rather shares an understanding of how they predicate themselves. Matrilineality is not simply a "trait," but, as the ingenious discussion of transformations demonstrates, it becomes as "maternal nurture" a moral force that informs even that *sanctum sanctorum* of Melanesian male sociality, the men's house. Perhaps, indeed, it was the very arbitrary quality of "matrilineality" (plus the pull of exoticism elsewhere), that led to the long neglect of New Ireland's peoples, for *Pinikindu* is only the second full-length published study dealing directly with a New Ireland sociality. By the same token, it is a signal achievement of Dr. Clay's study that Mandak maternal nurture is shown to be something more than an ethnographic fluke or the result of a jarring of the structural kaleidoscope. Both the usages of the Mandak and those of the neighboring Notsi (Lesu) emerge as (contrasting) motivated and coherent creations.

Finally, then, and most important of all, Dr. Clay's study embodies an approach to kin relations as a primarily *creative* (rather than a merely necessary) aspect of human life. So pervasive is the projected functionalism of our Western ideological interest, and so well-learned have been the tenets of its derivative "social anthropology," that even some of our best minds have taken "kinship" for granted as a dull and easily classified social building block. As an important locus of moral conception and motivation, kin relations provided the only acceptable surrogate for the kind of conscious collective order (not to speak of a "social contract") that generations of anthropologists were obliged to discover among the "primitives." The momentum of these "discoveries" is such that it often requires a good bit of "distancing" to realize that kin relations can be many things besides a mere social glue, or a tinkering with pedigrees. They can indeed focus the broad ambience of their creative interplay on the development of quite imaginative notions of nurturance or continuity, as they do among the Mandak. And since these foci involve a specifically human sort of generativeness, it can also be said that they imbue the acts of procreation and child-rearing, of affection and human interaction, with any meaning they may have, rather than take their sense and significance from them.

I should scarcely need to point out that the apprehension and delineation of such a creativity necessitates and implies a similar capacity in the analyst. I trust that readers will find Dr. Clay's book as rewarding and challenging an experience as I have found it.

Roy Wagner

Preface

Taking the air route from Port Moresby to Kavieng, New Ireland, via Lae, Goroka, Madang, Wewak, and Manus, gave me the impression I was progressively withdrawing into a brightly colored, clear, and noiseless corner of the universe. Quite dramatic is the contrast between the teeming, noisy airport in Port Moresby and the usual stillness of Kavieng. As an anthropologist in search of a "people," I must admit to feeling that I was running away from my subject when I disembarked from the airplane in Kavieng and two days later set off down the narrow east-coast road to look for housing among the Mandak-speakers. Yet in just a week my husband and I found ourselves settled in the midst of what was by no means a quiet or marginal village, but rather an intensely active group of people coping for better or worse with the complexities of life.

In June of 1970, my husband and I selected Pinikindu Village to be our residence among the Northern Mandak for the following eight months. The choice was based on a combination of factors. Pinikindu was attractive as a base for fieldwork because of its size, history, and settlement pattern. The village, with a population of 211, was relatively large by New Ireland standards and had been established as a Mandak settlement well before Western contact. Unlike many other east-coast villages, Pinikindu displayed the traditional settlement pattern of a number of separate hamlets. Because of the relatively short time I would be in New Ireland, I hoped to exclude for the present the complications caused by the resettlement of inland villages along the coast. The immediate availability of housing and the willingness of the villagers to have us live among them also influenced our choice of residence. Although all the villages we visited were hospitable, many did not have extra housing.

The house we moved into in Pinikindu was a partially completed Women's Club house. Within a few days after our arrival, villagers finished the house and modified it as they felt would best suit our purposes. Although we hoped that our residence would be somewhat neutral in social alignment, we soon discovered that it was definitely treated as part of the hamlet in which it was situated and that the Women's Club itself, an organization introduced by an American social worker in Kavieng, was nonoperative. We suggested to the village that we pay The Women's Club one dollar a day for the use of the house, hoping thereby to partially recompense the people for our presence. This arrangement was being used by another anthropologist, Dr. Phillip Lewis, in Lesu Village among the Notsi-speakers. It was successful for Dr. Lewis, since the Lesu Women's Club was actually functioning; among the Mandak, however, since the Women's Club existed in name only, our rent money was dispersed in several directions to individuals who made various claims on the house.

Before going to New Ireland, I had begun to learn Neo-Melanesian through tapes and workbooks. This preparation enabled me to pick up Neo-Melanesian rapidly once I was in New Ireland. My goal was to learn Mandak, but I did not succeed in becoming fluent in the local language before I left the field. Although most of my interviews were carried out in Neo-Melanesian, I conducted a number of sessions in Mandak. I always taped the latter conversations, since I never felt totally adequate in the language. Later the person interviewed would discuss the tapes and translate them into Neo-Melanesian. Although a few people in the village knew some English, no one was willing to speak it because of their uncertainty with the language and because doing so would exclude others from the conversation.

I more or less followed a general work schedule throughout my fieldwork. I would try to arrange a one- to three-hour interview session each day, for morning, afternoon, or evening depending on people's availability and preferences. These sessions took place either in our house or in the person's hamlet. I spent the rest of each day in general participant observation. Day-to-day work schedules, however, were rather variable, owing to crises or to special activities or feasts.

The problem of establishing an appropriate social identity for myself in the community had to be solved in the early stages of my fieldwork. Here was a culture which separated male and female in work and in socializing. When we first arrived people tried to fit me completely into the female realm of activities and my husband into the men's area of interests and associations. However, I felt I had to reject such a position since I did not want to work only with the women, who had little time for lengthy discussions because they were busy with gardening, cooking, and child care. Since they had less experience in dealing with outsiders, women were also reticent in talking to strangers and not as adept as men in articulating their own culture. For these reasons I worked primarily, although not exclusively, with men in interviews and lengthy discussions.

It took a certain amount of explanation to convince people that during much of the day I had to occupy an essentially male role—in the task of "interviewing." Whereas women were generally engaged in gardening and domestic tasks, it was not unusual for men to sit and talk among themselves for long periods in the afternoon. I explained that the government and school which financed my trip to New Ireland expected me to accumulate data on both male and female areas of knowledge. These explanations were generally accepted and throughout most of the fieldwork period I had no difficulty in questioning either sex. On all formal feasting occasions I was identified with the women in the female area of the hamlet, while my husband remained in the men's house. I was satisfied with the identity into which I eventually settled, associating with the women during feasting and ceremonial occasions but having access to either sexual sphere during the daily routines. The formal association with the women was necessary if I was to have rapport with them and be accepted as a "person" by the village. The informal "neutrality" was also essential if I was to have access to data from men and to perceive the culture from several viewpoints.

Before we went to New Ireland, anthropologists in Port Moresby informed us that they had heard that the people of New Ireland were extremely congenial to visitors, but that they had "lost their culture" in acculturated pursuit of the coconut. Despite this latter misinformation, we found the former to be quite true. The Mandak were an extremely pleasant people for an anthropologist to work with. They never appeared to resent our presence. They wanted us, as much as possible, to take part in their daily routines, and they always made sure we were invited to their feasts and special events. A generally egalitarian relationship was soon established between us and the Mandak, in accordance with our mutual social preferences. The Mandak retained a degree of superiority in assuming the roles of "teacher" and "host" to our complementary position as "students" and "guests." Throughout our stay they treated us with good-humored tolerance, patience, and a certain curiosity. In summary, fieldwork among the Mandak was a gentle and kindly introduction to a culture different from my own.

Although I cannot include here all the Mandak individuals who contributed to this study, I would like to mention some of them. Particularly, I am grateful to Ulimat, Darus, and Ruth of Lembe; Mumurandan of Udua; Mogolomen, Damot, Marwus, and Nonobin of Lekelieu; Paulo, Aida, and Wakendak of Kaluan I; Wakamba of Malambo; Ransu of Kasasambwang; Timot, Kougo and Kararara of Tuwaram; and Leleang of Katenbanema. Ligidak of Udua was a particularly valuable assistant and friend. Various children enlivened our stay, especially Kristen, Engleberd, Towira, Wilfred, and Lyon.

Of special importance to this study has been the assistance of Francis Luttam, whose knowledge, appreciation, and articulations of his own culture have been of invaluable aid. As my *tamak*, Francis contributed to the development of my understanding and to my general wellbeing in Pinikindu.

This book is a revision of my doctoral dissertation (August 1974) in anthropology at Southern Illinois University, Carbondale, Illinois. My fieldwork in New Ireland was financed by a doctoral dissertation grant from the National Science Foundation (1970–71) and by Southern Illinois University through the Graduate Development Fund and a special doctoral assistantship. I am grateful to Dr. Philip Dark both for his extensive advice in preparation for fieldwork and for his encouragement and helpful criticisms while I was writing this study. I also extend thanks for additional suggestions and criticisms which were offered me at various stages of writing by Drs. Peter Munch, Jerome Handler, and Joel Maring.

During our first week in New Ireland, while we were looking for a resident village, we were the guests of Dr. Phillip Lewis, who was spending the year (1969–70) at Lesu Village among the Notsispeakers. Many times since then we have congratulated the circumstances which allowed our mutual residence in New Ireland, for Dr. Lewis proved to be a most congenial and helpful neighbor. He assisted us throughout our stay and afterward in many ways, from accommodating us during Notsi feasts to sharing his own translations of German ethnographical materials.

The writings and ideas of Dr. Roy Wagner have been a major source of "nurture" to my theoretical position and general approach to anthropology. Dr. Wagner was kind enough to comment on my field notes while I was in New Ireland. My interest in cultural symbols derives directly from his writings, particularly *Habu* (1972), although responsibility for their use in this book is my own. Throughout the analysis and writing of this study, his ideas and influence have been stimulating in a general sense and his particular criticisms greatly appreciated.

The other half of the "we" in this study is my husband, Dr. R. Berle Clay. Not only was he willing to take leave from his own work to go to New Ireland, but from the moment our plane left California, his enthusiasm for Papua New Guinea and the Mandak people was an unsolicited boost to my fieldwork. In addition to moral support and actual help in the field, he has also contributed to my knowledge of the Mandak by his archaeological reconnaisance of the area, his analysis of settlement patterns, and his help in linguistic analysis of the Northern Mandak dialect. I am also grateful for his work in preparing maps 1 and 2.

Finally, I thank my small sons, Torsten and Severn, for sharing their own "nurture" with the writing of this study.

Throughout this book when I refer to the Mandak people I am discussing only the Northern Mandak who occupy the villages of Lawatbura, Pinikindu, Sominim, Konos, and Lamusong. Although many of the data from the Northern Mandak are applicable to the Southern, West-Coast, and Lelet Plateau Mandak, there are also cultural differences between these groups. As a simplification, I have omitted the "Northern" preface in my use of "Mandak."

As an additional simplification, I have formed the plural of most Mandak words by adding the English suffix "-s" or "-es" rather than by the more complicated Mandak procedures. All Mandak terms cited in the text follow the linguistic forms used in Pinikindu Village. There are linguistic differences from village to village within the Northern Mandak dialect area.

All monetary values mentioned refer to Australian currency. In 1971, the exchange rate was Australian $1.00 for United States $1.1585.

Introduction

The language of poetry expresses condensed, texturally loaded meaning, often through metaphor, symbol, simile, and metonymy. Through both familiar and novel images, the poet conveys the emotional and conceptual force of his medium. Although poetry may intensify our awareness of the communicative power of metaphor, particularly through innovative and provocative associations, symbolization is also a process through which cultural traditions are created and maintained. A poem, as expressive art, may momentarily juxtapose images or concepts; and as members of social groups we create and share our understandings through the same symbolizing process. The resulting cultural concepts, however, are not the temporary extensions of poetry, for they form the core of significations through which we perceive ourselves and our surroundings. As members of social groups, we are all poets with the potential to extend our understandings and worlds through innovative symbolization; but we are also constrained and limited within cultural traditions which are both the boundaries of our perceptions and the matrix and wellspring of our apperceptions.

This study is an interpretative analysis of cultural symbolizations of the Mandak people of central New Ireland, Papua New Guinea. The symbols that will be discussed are those through which the Mandak define and articulate interpersonal and intergroup relationships. My interests focus on the significations communicated and expressed in Mandak major social distinctions. Such meanings are actualized through shared metaphorical associations which shape and signify important cultural understandings. I will be concerned with cultural meanings communicated by the Mandak, not with observations based on statistical occurrences of actual social interactions.

"Symbol" is used here in the sense of metaphor, involving a particular kind of relationship between two or more separable entities. The relationship between elements of a symbolic construction is not arbitrary, a matter of established convention, like a sign, where the letter A stands for a group of vocal sounds. The association between elements of a symbol involves a measure both of similarity and of difference. In a recent study, Wagner discusses this aspect of a cultural symbol.[1]

> Nontautologous meaning can only be produced through the innovative extension of signifiers into metaphors, that is, the formation of symbols whose contrast with the element signified is supplemented by a relation of similarity, or analogy, with that element. Thus although lexical signification is characterized by an arbitrary relationship between signifier and signified, metaphorical signification involves a nonarbitrary and determinate relationship between signifier and signified. The key to this difference is the fact of relationship itself; a metaphor brings the element signified into relation with the system of meanings in a culture, whereas lexical signification merely registers its conventions of labeling. A lexical "coding" signifies an isolated element, but a metaphor signifies a relation.[2]

A cultural symbol is neither a superficial signification nor an artificial embellishment of "reality." Metaphorization is not a cultural process whereby a neutral world is organized for communicative purposes, for both the elements of symbolic constructions and the resulting metaphoric meaning are phenomena of cultural perceptions. Thus no contrast exists between the "symbolic" and the "real," but only manifestations of different cultural worlds. When we say a gesture is "symbolic," we often imply that the act is somehow a counterfeit of reality; that it is merely representative of something more significant. It is difficult to comprehend the realities of other people's symbols because in cross-cultural perspective we always perceive "their" world through our own and thus we explicitly or implicitly contrast the two, granting a "truth" to our own perceptions and attributing artificiality to theirs. To define a reality as "only" a cultural perception does not in any way denigrate it but simply acknowledges the source, creativity, and complexity of its meaning.

The cultural symbolizations which are the focus of this study are not mere representations to the Mandak. When a person expresses a symbol in a particular context, he is not performing an act which "stands for" something else: rather his actions *are* the communicated meaning of his experience. For example, associated elements of a Mandak symbolization are "female" and "provision of sustenance." After giving birth, a woman performs the ritual of feeding her infant masticated taro. This woman's gesture is symbolic to the Mandak. The gesture does not merely represent something; it *is* one form of the metaphorization of female and the provision of sustenance. The form is recreated again and again by individual females after giving birth. Other symbolic expressions relevant to this symbolization define the meaning of the woman's action, which in turn contributes to the significations of other contexts. A symbolic expression is the actualization rather than the representation of people's shared understandings.

"Symbol" refers to the anthropologist's analytic terms which interpret and objectify another culture's symbolizations. I will use the latter term, "symbolization," to refer directly to people's expressions of their shared metaphors. "Form" and "expression" are synonymous terms indicating the actual communication of a symbolization—the words, gestures, and signs which convey symbolic meaning. A "symbolic idiom" is an element or a significant part of a symbolization which is expressed or manifested in numerous contexts. The same contrasts and associations are found in my symbols, I suggest, and in the Mandak symbolizations they interpret; but the symbols, as translations and objectifications, involve selection, simplification, and a measure of my own cultural filter of explanation. Selection was guided by features which I viewed as significant to the Mandak, which they emphasized in their discussions to me, and which were reiterated and elaborated in multiple contexts.

The process of cultural symbolization is continuous and cumulative. It is difficult to truly isolate discrete cultural symbols, for their significations are derived from accumulated associations reiterated in multiple contexts. "Context" refers to the immediate environment of a symbolic form or expression, to the gestures, ritual apparatus, spatial requirements, and so forth, which are necessary for people to recognize the context. Since any single context may contain a number of diverse symbolic expressions, descriptions of contextual features of a symbolic expression may differ according to the focus of the symbolic form. I will use "context," unless otherwise indicated, to refer to contexts with different contents rather than to the individual occurrences of a context.

Because in every individual action a symbolic association may be created, recreated, or modified, and because symbolizations exist through their actualization in particular contexts, the process of

cultural creativity is ongoing and continual. In their daily interactions and their ceremonial expressions, people do not simply
attune their behavior to an ideal model of symbolization. Their
actions are motivated by shared understandings, which in turn are
continually reshaped and extended through individual expressions.
There are, of course, varying degrees of symbolic modification in
any social group. From day-to-day variations in symbolic expression, there are points at which a noticeable shift in emphasis or
creativity will effect a major difference in symbolic pattern. In the
course of contact with Asian and European cultures, the Mandak
have both lost and added certain expressive forms of symbolizations. Although certainly the Mandak have changed in many ways
since precontact days, I suggest that the major distinctions and
contrasts which structure their symbolizations have not changed in
any radical direction within their known past.

Recognizing the relativity of cultural worlds, an approach concerned with symbolic analysis must define its investigative perimeters only in general terms in order to allow the "data" to move in
directions ordained by its creators and not by the analytic terms. An
example of the sterile results produced by imposing a predefined
domain on cultural investigations is the domination of "kinship"
analyses by the constrictive genealogical framework.[3] We cannot
merely examine diverse cultural views of *our* world; in each analysis
the shape of the world itself must be uncovered.

In general terms, therefore, the focus of this study of Mandak
social symbols is an attempt to understand the major symbolizations
through which these people define and articulate their social
relationships. What meanings do the Mandak express about their
shared social distinctions? What differences and similarities between persons determine or are the products of interpersonal and
intergroup relationships? My answers to these questions are presented and organized through a pattern of symbols which I call
nurture, maternal nurture, paternal substance, and *affinal nurture.*
These symbols do not interpret the total social environment of the
Mandak, but I suggest that they synthesize major symbolizations
expressed in Mandak social relationships. In a sense, the nurture
symbols describe "primary" Mandak symbolizations, in that other
kinds of social interactions occur within or through relationships
which are determined by and expressive of these symbolizations. For
example, Mandak political interactions work through relationships
which express various aspects of the nurture symbols.

Symbolic meaning is produced through a conceptual relationship recognized between elements. The parts of a metaphoric construction are not associated by mere addition: the integration of concepts produces meaning different from that of either element. Thus the symbol I call "nurture" involves an association of procreative concepts with the provision of sustenance, wealth, support, protection, and anything else that sustains life. The cultural meaning of nurture is not the result of a mere representation of procreation as nurture, or vice versa, but derives from a complex metaphorization of procreation and nurture in which the two concepts are brought together to form a signification different from a mere conjunction of separate ideas. The terms used here, "procreation" and "nurture," are glosses for complex Mandak concepts: a more complete explication of nurture as a symbol will be given later. However, it is important at this point to emphasize that the Mandak cultural symbols are the expressive and understood reality of their world and that these symbols are not mere products of conceptual additions.

The nurture symbols are derived from numerous expressions of symbolizations in many different contexts. In each context, a symbolization is manifested, created, and expressed in slightly different form, and the many diverse forms together make up the symbol's signification. The links between contextual forms relevant to a symbol may be features of redundancy or opposition, or various forms of analogy. My interpretive symbols, therefore, are syntheses of meanings derived from conceptually interrelated contexts. The symbol of maternal nurture, for example, entails symbolic associations between female, "being of one kind," taro, same social unit, and sharing. The actual contexts in which maternal nurture forms are manifested are as diverse as a woman planting taro; a taro harvest feast within the men's house; a woman nursing a baby; and a woman taking food to the household of her male sibling. Each of these contexts assumes its meaning from the others and in turn helps create the symbolization of maternal nurture.

In my attempt to understand Mandak symbolizations of interpersonal and intergroup relationships, I found significant symbolic expressions in many different areas of Mandak life, such as normative definitions of social relationships; spatial patterns and conceptualizations; the organization of activities and work; contrasts between human and "nonhuman" beings; myths; feasting and ceremonial events; and formal and informal reciprocal interactions. Because the nurture symbolizations are so pervasive in Mandak social interactions, there is probably no area of culture which would not add something to this inquiry. The general cultural concerns around which I have organized my analysis and presentation include: social categories, a group of mutually interdependent social relationships which are the primary means for the interpersonal articulation of distinctions of nurture; the sexual dichotomy, one of the major distinctions of nurturing relationships; and reciprocal interactions, another major differentiating form of nurture.

The nurture symbols are part of a symbolic "pattern" in that the meaning of any one symbol depends on its relationship to other symbols in the pattern. The interrelationships are not imposed on the symbols because they are all involved with social distinctions, for the connections between symbols, whether of opposition or complementarity, are created, reiterated, and shared as part of the symbolic meanings. For example, the Mandak expressly contrast a person's reciprocal interactions with his father and those with his mother: a person exchanges with his father, shares with his mother. In the contexts of these interrelationships, the symbolic elements of sharing/exchanging are brought into a comparative relation and deliberately contrasted.

The relationships between the nurture symbols are thus formulated as syntheses of multiple contrasts and comparisons of symbolic forms within specific contexts. "Female," for example, is part of a complex symbolization which metaphorically incorporates sharing, same social unit, "being of one kind," taro, and many other features. These associations are reiterated in variant forms in different contexts to create the symbolization I call "maternal nurture." This symbol is related to the paternal substance symbol through the numerous contexts which contrast or complementarize male/female, exchanging/sharing, same social unit/cross-social unit. These symbolic contrasts are not, however, static oppositions, for they combine in various relations of contrast or complementarity in different contexts. Thus, in certain situations expressions of maternal nurture and paternal substance combine to oppose forms of a symbolization I call "affinal nurture." The relationships between symbols, therefore, are not merely hypothesized because they are all relevant to social distinctions; rather, the connections are expressed within the contexts and are aspects of the symbolic significations.

The meaning of a symbolic pattern is not conveyed solely through the metaphorizations and their relationships of opposition, complementarity, or contradiction. From a broader perspective, symbolic significations are also derived from a people's focus on certain modes of articulation between symbols and also on a general kind of implicit commitment to the symbolizations. These aspects of symbolic meaning are subtle and complex, but they must be considered before we can understand the ways in which cultural meaning is implemented in social interactions.

The pattern of symbols that emerges in this study involves differentiation of symbols through opposition or complementarity. In the nurture pattern, the major symbols of maternal nurture, paternal substance, and affinal nurture are essentially differentiating symbols which mutually define one another through contrasting and complementary relationships. Nurture is the focal symbol within this pattern. A "focal symbol" incorporates and synthesizes numerous differentiating symbols. A focal symbol "contains" and, in a conceptual sense, negates its differential parts. As a social symbolization, therefore, the focal symbol serves as a collective and socially integrating expression. As I will discuss later, the Mandak cultural tradition involves an emphasis on the differentiating symbols of social relationships, while the similarities between distinctions are implied rather than directly articulated. In one sense, the focal symbol of nurture is created through the forms of the major symbols: it is mediated through its contrasting forms. Although the focal symbol of nurture is conceptually integrating, it does not serve explicitly in expressive form to generalize human relationships. Instead, nurture is an understood residue, a background of similarities of the expressed differences.

In the chapters that follow, the significations of the Mandak nurture symbols will be gradually developed and explicated. I hope to explore not merely the content of Mandak symbolizations but, more important, the processes through which such cultural significations are expressed and the way meaning is generated within a symbolic pattern.

I hope that the nurture symbols presented here will convey in a meaningful way certain basic concepts the Mandak share about human relationships. This analysis necessarily imparts an artificiality to the Mandak symbolizations. Because they are dissected and objectified as "symbols," Mandak concepts assume a less than real appearance for the reader. Unfortunately, such is the correlate of cross-cultural explication; but I still regret that I could not communicate in less synthetic form the texturally rich and interesting creations of the Mandak people.

People of the Sea

Situated between 2 and 5 degrees south latitude and between 150 and 154 degrees east longitude, New Ireland is a coral reef fringed island of the Bismarck Archipelago. The New Ireland District comprises, in addition to New Ireland itself, the smaller islands of Lavongai (New Hanover), the Saint Matthias group, Tabar, Lihir, Tanga, and Feni. New Ireland is a land mass of 3,340 square miles, 220 miles in length, varying in width from 7 to 35 miles. Formed from the tops of submerged mountain ranges running parallel to the Central Cordillera of New Guinea, the island begins in its northern extremity with the quiet harbor town of Kavieng (1969 population about 1,165), proceeds south through low-lying country to the foothills of the Schlientz ranges in the north-central interior, then runs to the more rugged heights of Lelet Plateau (3,000′) in the central area. Here the island widens to about 16 miles, only to narrow again around the small settlement of Namatanai, 170 miles south of Kavieng. Farther south the land broadens to its maximum width of 35 miles, while the coastal plains narrow and the interior mountains descend steeply into the sea. In the southern part of the island, the highest peak of the Rossel ranges is 6,430′.

New Ireland's population today is concentrated along the coasts. The settlements are larger and more densely populated in the northeast between Kavieng and Namatanai, but become sparser along the west coast, and still smaller and more scattered in the extreme southern areas. The only interior settlement is on Lelet Plateau, which in 1970 had a population of about 500. New Ireland's settlement pattern has not always reflected the present coastal concentration, a result of geographic features and Western contact. When the German administration (1884–1914) had the coral-surfaced road built along the east coast from Kavieng to ten miles south of Namatanai, they began the resettlement of inland villages along the coast. In addition, the relatively wide coastal plains in the northeast afford more space for population concentration than the rougher interior and the narrower confines of the west coast and the east coast south of Namatanai.

New Ireland is tropical in climate and vegetation. The climate reflects a contrast: a wet season dominated by the northwest monsoon winds from December to May and a dry season influenced by southeast trade winds from May to October, divided by transitional calmer, more humid weather. However, rainfall may vary considerably according to local topographic features. For example, Pinikindu peninsula is an exceptionally dry finger of land jutting out from wetter environs five miles north and south. Drought remains an annual threat to Pinikindu village from May to October, which we found could be dry indeed. There is little change in mean monthly temperatures, which range from the high seventies to about ninety degrees.

Along low coastal areas of the northern and central areas of the island, the present vegetation reflects man's presence by extensive stands of coconut palms, interspersed with areca palms, and bamboo trees. Lowland tropical forest appears in the more rugged coastal areas beginning some twenty miles north of Namatanai. Intermittent mangrove swamps of tidal and saline mud flats are also found in the north to central areas, while farther south, narrow, clear, rapid rivers descend from interior mountain ranges extending almost to the coast. In the higher interior areas, midmontane forest and lowland rain forests predominate, the mountainous areas being covered by dense forests, tall, often flange-based semideciduous trees, and vast stands of wild bamboo shading moist moss-covered, slippery, and rocky terrain.

The Mandak

In central New Ireland live the Mandak, a cultural-linguistic group of Melanesian peoples (map 1). "Mandak" derives from their term for "male" (Northern Mandak *emandak*) and is used by the New Irelanders themselves to refer to peoples speaking the Mandak language. In a recent linguistic survey of New Ireland, this language is called "Madak."[1] I will use the local variant, "Mandak." This book is concerned with the Northern Mandak who constitute the dialect group occupying the villages of Lawatbura to Lamusong on the east coast (map 2). The Mandak language is Austronesian, spoken by a population of 3,325.[2] Lithgow and Claasen divide the

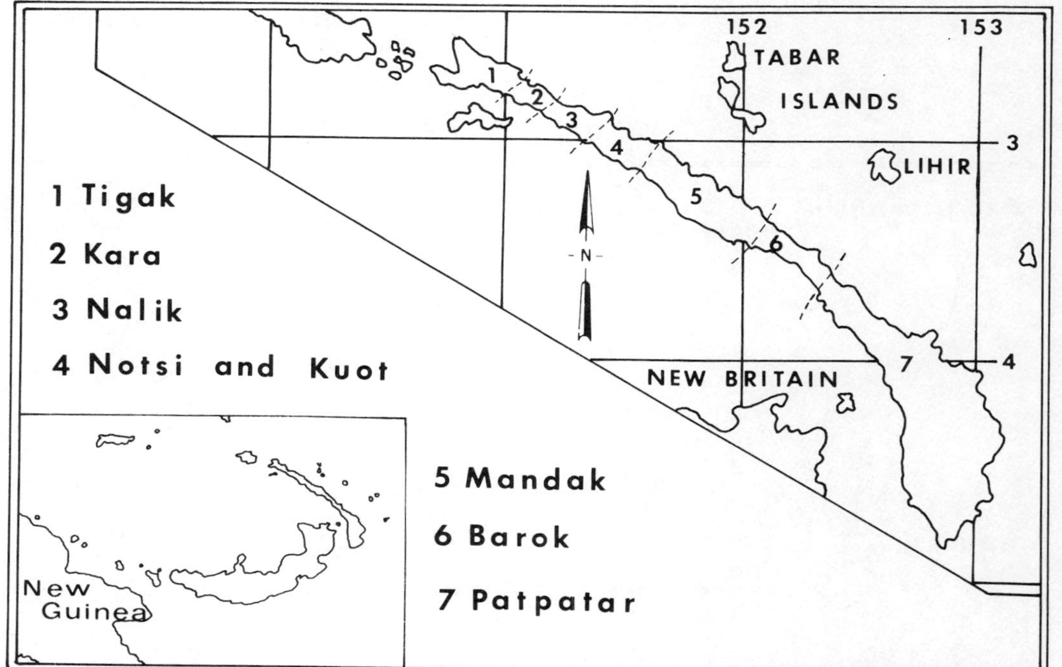

Map 1. Linguistic subdivisions of New Ireland. *Sources*: Phillip H. Lewis, *The Social Context of Art in Northern New Ireland*, p. 29; David Lithgow and Orev Claasen, *Languages of the New Ireland District*; and the Northern Mandak.

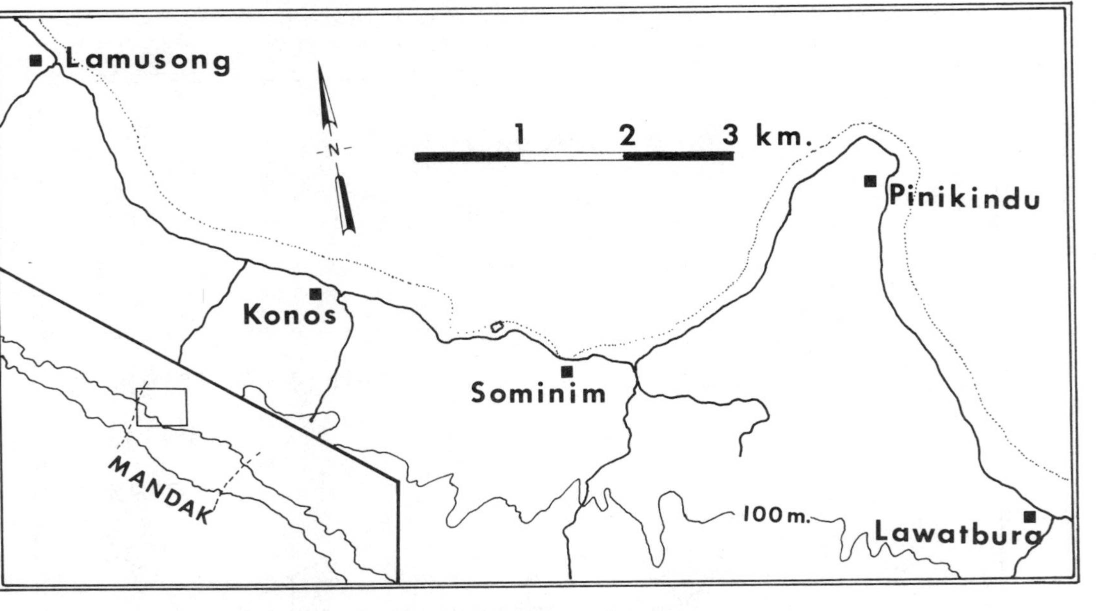

Map 2. The Northern Mandak

Madak family into *Madak* (2,031 speakers), comprising five dialects: Malom and Katingan on the east coast, Mesi and Danu on the west coast, Lelet in the interior; and the *Lamusong-Lavatbura* family (1,293 speakers), comprising four dialects: Lamusong and Lawatbura on the east coast, Kontu and Ugana on the west coast.[3] The Northern Mandak include the Lamusong and Lawatbura dialect groups of Lithgow and Claasen's classification.

The Mandak are relatively tall and well built, not uncommon for Melanesian coastal populations. The predominant skin color is medium brown, often with reddish tones. Continuing an island tradition, most people peroxide their rather shortly cut hair to a light yellow, while some dye their hair black or reddish brown. Only old women and men older than about forty leave their hair its natural brown. The custom derives from precontact days, when the distinctive blond appearance was achieved by dusting the hair with powdered lime. Women may also enhance their appearance with facial tattoos.

The Northern Mandak constitute a cultural unit in that they see themselves as sharing a core of customs which distinguishes them from other dialect groups. The smallest culturally differentiated social group is the village, which unites under one name a number of contiguous hamlets. Each village is distinguished from others not only by dialectal details, but also by cultural specialities, minor rituals, ceremonial features, or technological skills. A larger cultural division includes several villages sharing the same dialect. Within such groups, however, are recognized distinctions between coastal and inland peoples. Of the Northern Mandak villages, Lamusong and Pinikindu are traditionally coastal, while Lawatbura (formerly Tegero), Sominim (formerly Konobin), and Konos were once in hilly, semimountainous areas several miles from the sea. In the first decade of the twentieth century the Germans began to move inland peoples to coastal locations, and the Australians completed this resettlement in the early 1950s. Although many cultural differences between coastal and inland groups have disappeared, minor variations in custom and outlook continue. In some instances, for example recent council elections, the Northern Mandak divide into coastal and inland factions. I will be concerned with the coastal culture, which is generally shared today by the former inland villages.

Let me summarize the different levels of sociocultural identification by the varying contrasts typically made by a Pinikindu man.

Such a person may at one level identify himself as a man of Pinikindu village in contrast to a person of Lamusong village. In other contexts he may group himself with the coastal villages, Pinikindu and Lamusong, as distinct from the precontact bush villages, Konos, Sominim, and Lawatbura. At yet another level, he contrasts himself as a speaker of Northern Mandak to the southern speakers of "true" Mandak, while in a more inclusive context he identifies himself as Mandak, in contrast to the neighboring Notsi, Kuot, and Barok language groups.

A further sociocultural distinction is being introduced today in New Ireland by the government census divisions, which do not always reiterate traditional cultural-linguistic groups. The Northern Mandak are included in the Notsi-Mandak Census Division of the Central New Ireland District, which incorporates fourteen villages from Tandes to Lambuso, in the area from Daskigi Plantation to Kimidan on the east coast.

During my residence in New Ireland from June 1970 through January 1971, my husband and I lived in a Kaluan clan hamlet in Pinikindu village. Much of my information was obtained from the people of our resident village, although I also interviewed other Northern Mandak speakers and attended feasts and events in several different villages. Pinikindu has been situated in its present location at least since earliest Western contact. An archaeological test excavation in the village indicates human occupation of the area as far back as about 300 B.C., although these early residents were pottery-making peoples, an art not practiced by the historically know Mandak.[4]

In 1970, Pinikindu comprised twenty-four hamlets strung along a peninsula jutting out from the east coast, ninety-six miles south of Kavieng and seventy-four miles north of Namatanai (map 3). The population in 1970 was 211, a decrease from the 245 reported in 1929.[5] A striking population decline occurred throughout much of New Ireland from about 1910 to 1950, after which the population began to stabilize and in some areas to increase. A recent study suggests that the low fertility was due to the debilitating effects of widespread gonorrhea introduced by Western contact.[6] At present, census figures for central New Ireland indicate that the population is slowly increasing.

Previous ethnographic work in New Ireland includes the studies done in the early 1900s by George Friederici, Augustin Kramer, Elisabeth Kramer-Bannow, Richard Parkinson, P. Gerhard Peekel,

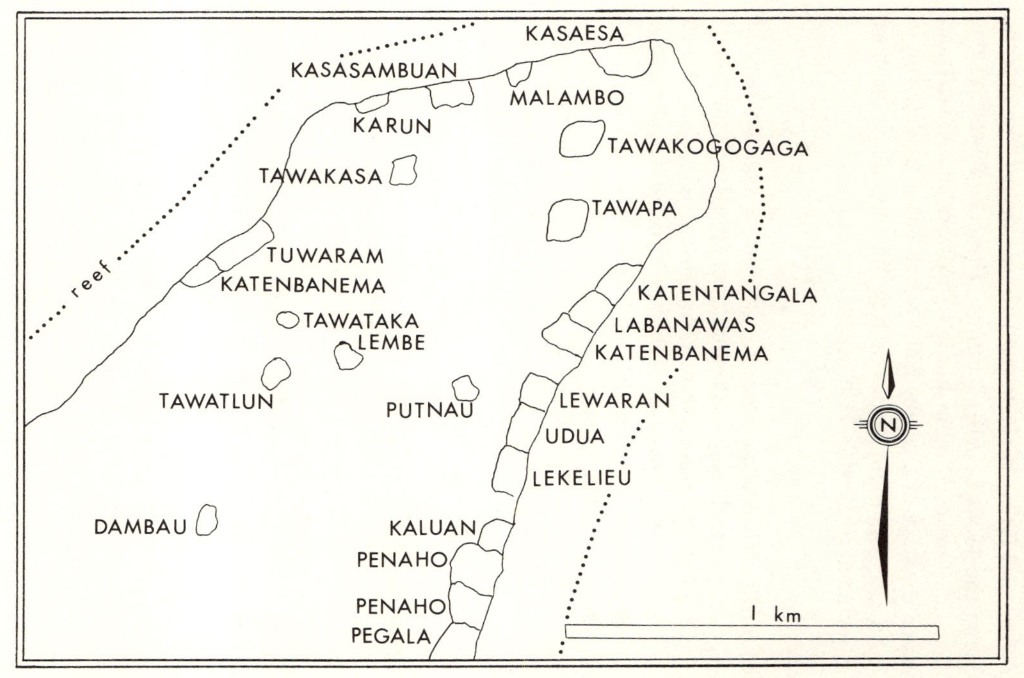

Map 3. Hamlets in Pinikindu Village: 1970

Emil Stephen, and Edgar Walden; the 1929 survey by Chinnery; the work done in the 1930s by Alfred Buhler, Hortense Powdermaker, and William C. Groves; Phillip Lewis's fieldwork in 1953–54 and 1969–70; and the work of Dorothy Billings and Nicholas Peterson in 1966–67. An extensive bibliography on New Ireland and its offshore islands is included in Lewis's 1969 study.

Economy

The Mandak subsistence economy involves a combination of shifting agriculture and fishing. Predominant crops and fruit plants include taro, sweet potatoes, yams, bananas, beans, leafy green vegetables, pineapples, papayas, melons, breadfruit, oranges, pandanus, and a variety of nuts. Also grown in small quantities are tobacco, maize, and sugarcane. Although sago palms grow in central New Ireland, the Northern Mandak no longer produce sago for food; instead they occasionally obtain it from villages to the north. Taro and sweet potatoes form the bulk of their daily diet, supplemented by greens, various fruits, and fish. The people practice slash-and-burn agriculture to clear new gardens from secondary forest one-half to three miles from the coast. Approximately eight months elapse between the planting of the tops of taro plants and the tuber's harvest. Usually only one crop is planted in a garden, although plantings are staggered so that each garden is used for about one and a half years then allowed to lie fallow for two to three years before it is replanted in taro or sweet potato. Sweet potatoes are sometimes grown in a garden immediately after a taro crop is harvested. Sweet potatoes take about six months to mature, and two successive crops are generally grown in the same garden. The only tools used in gardening are the bush knife and digging stick.

The sea, yielding shellfish, sea turtles, and many varieties of fish, provides much of the protein in the Mandak diet. It is difficult to estimate the extent of dependence on the sea for food, for there is much variation from hamlet to hamlet in weekly consumption of fish. I observed that some households supplemented their meals with seafood only once a week while others ate fish at least three or four times a week.

A variety of fishing methods were used in 1970–71. In one form of group fishing about twelve men walk in waist-deep water and by beating the water with sticks and shouting drive fish into some thirty feet of net held by six to ten men. The fish are then speared or caught in the net and thrown into a waiting canoe. In another group effort, five to eight men scare fish into a pile of stones which have been placed within the reef, ten to fifteen yards from shore. With nets the men circle in on the stones and remove them while spearing or netting the fish. Individual fishing methods include spearfishing within the reef by day or at night by torchlight; Western hook-and-line fishing from shore or canoe; spearfishing for large fish beyond the reef from a canoe or by swimming; and fish poisoning—various poisonous roots are chewed and spit out into shallow pools within the reef. Elaborate techniques were once used in shark-catching expeditions, but these have not taken place for the past twenty years, although sharks are still speared when they are attracted within the reef by the blood of slaughtered pigs or fish. Fishing equipment now used includes locally carved single-outrigger dugout canoes; spears with Western- or Asian-manufactured iron points; locally made or Western- or Asian-produced nets with shell sinkers and carved wooden floats; Western- or Asian-made hooks and lines; and Asian-produced goggles for underwater fishing.

An additional source of protein in Mandak diets is wild and domesticated animals. The former include pigs, cuscus, various lizards, and birds, all of which are hunted in the inland hills and mountains. However, hunting is not a frequent occupation. The Mandak raise pigs and chickens or purchase them from other villages. Domestic pigs are important items of exchange and wealth and are eaten only in connection with feasting and exchange. By government regulation pigs are kept in fenced areas away from the villages. Chickens are free-roaming scavengers; they are eaten infrequently and usually not within any particular social context. Several small to medium-sized dogs are kept by many hamlets for pig hunting and to give alarm against lurking sorcerers.

The subsistence agricultural and fishing economy has long been supplemented by Western or Asian market products bought with money from the sale of copra and cocoa. Cocoa is a recently introduced cash crop, but the Mandak have had their own coconut plantations since the early 1950s. The Germans and English first introduced copra marketing in the area in the late nineteenth century. Many Mandak men worked on European-owned plantations until the late 1940s, then they began to concentrate on their own cash crops while the European managers found cheaper labor in the newly contacted areas of New Guinea. The income per family from the sale of copra and cocoa may reach $500 to $600 annually.

With the cash obtained by selling copra and cocoa and by occasional wage labor for Europeans, as boss-boys on nearby plantations or dockworkers for alien ships, the Mandak buy a number of Western and Asian products. The most common food purchases include canned meats and fish, rice, tea, bread, coffee, biscuits and sugar. They also buy cigarettes and beer. While all these items may at times supplement daily meals, the Mandak do not prefer them over the traditional diet of taro, sweet potato, and fresh fish. People regard rice and canned fish, for example, as occasional time-saving substitutes which lack the taste and energy-giving qualities of their traditional foods.

Manufactured articles bought from Kavieng, Namatanai, or trade trucks include laplaps, shirts, blouses, belts, men's Western-style short pants, kerosene and pressure lamps, knives, flashlights, cigarette lighters, dishes, spoons, kettles, kerosene stoves, and radios. Everyone wears manufactured clothing: laplaps for both sexes, and—for "dress" or protection against wet weather—shirts for men and blouses for women. Within each village a few individuals own bicycles, which they may rent to other people; and usually one hamlet in each village owns a truck which is hired out to carry people, copra, and cocoa to Kavieng or Namatanai markets.

The traditional medium of exchange among the Mandak is strands of shell-disks. One variety, *evenugun*, was manufactured in the Pinikindu area, while others, the sources unknown, were obtained in trade and circulated throughout New Ireland, Lihir, Tabar, Buka, and New Hanover. Today the supply is limited since shell beads are no longer being made in any of these areas. Except for evenugun, of minimal value since the 1950s when the paramount Luluai, Bukbuk of Penatkin, forbade its use in feast exchanges, people carefully guard their shell valuables. The dogs'-teeth necklace, *ewakandu*, traditionally served as a mark of future exchange obligations, although today it has been replaced by the Australian shilling. Many, if not most, Mandak exchanges involve combinations of shell beads and Australian currency.

Some technological specialization occurs from village to village. In Pinikindu, for example, people are still known for making a type of shell arm bracelet, *emelot*, which they occasionally use for decoration themselves but more often trade to peoples farther south in exchange for shell beads. Although some individuals within each village are noted for their technological skills, age and sex are the only criteria for manufacturing roles. Older males make shell bracelets and shell pendants, polish beads, carve canoes, make fishnets and floats, and manufacture various minor ceremonial items. Carving dance masks, however, is a special skill of only a few men. Any adult male may make his own palm-frond basket, just as any adult woman generally produces her own lime pouches, rain covers, sleeping mats, and palm-frond baskets.

In precontact times the coastal and inland villages of central New Ireland engaged in a regular trade of food products. Pinikindu, for example, traded with the inland villages of Konobin and Tegero. Such trade was conducted solely by women, since warfare hostilities generally kept men of different villages wary of one another. At set neutral locations, women from bush hamlets traded taro, green vegetables, tobacco, yams, sugarcane, betel, and occasionally pieces of wild pig to the coastal women for seaweed, salt, fish, and coconuts. This trade ended in the early 1950s after all inland hamlets had resettled along the coast. Today, however, women still do the trading in the weekly vegetable markets in Kavieng and Namatanai, where they sell taro, sweet potato, vegetables, and fruits. Since the Mandak live some eighty to one hundred miles from either town, trade is infrequent, carried on perhaps once a month by a few women from each village, who must hire a truck to carry themselves and their produce to market.

SOCIAL GROUPS AND SETTLEMENT PATTERN

Although this book focuses on Mandak social distinctions, let me briefly introduce some general features of their social organization. From the Notsi-speakers in central New Ireland throughout the remainder of the island to the south are found matrilineal, exogamous moieties. The dual divisions contain exogamous matrilineal clans which may be further subdivided into subclans and sub-subclans. Throughout this area, moieties are named after birds: in Pinikindu, two types of sea eagles called *Emalam* and *Erangam*. *Ebibinet* is the Pinikindu term for clan, while *ewentus* denotes both subclan and sub-subclan divisions. North of the Notsi villages, exogamous matrilineal clans occur without dual organization.

In precontact times, New Ireland villages within and across language areas interacted through warfare, intermarriages, feasting, and trading. The Mandak described the past tenor of intervillage relationships as hostile, involving recurrent fighting. The preferred form of marriage, past and present, is within the village. Present marriages recorded from Pinikindu, however, indicated that only about half of actual marriages are made within the village.[7] The same clans may be represented in different villages in a dialect group and to a smaller extent in neighboring language groups. In Pinikindu village in 1970–71, nineteen Erangam clans and fifteen Emalam clans were represented.

Intervillage communication has no doubt increased since the Germans put an end to local hostilities in the early twentieth century, since the east coast road was built, and since modern transportation—trucks, buses, and bicycles—has been introduced. Pinikindu residents attend feasts in villages ten to thirty or more miles to the south and north along the east coast, and also in the more inaccessible areas of the west coast, although they rarely visit hamlets on Lelet Plateau. A bus service from Kavieng to Namatanai, begun in 1969, provides an increasingly popular means of transportation along the east coast.

The Mandak use land mainly for gardens and homesites. Houses are grouped together as hamlets within villages and generally are apart from the gardens, which are one-half to three miles inland from coastal villages. In Pinikindu, for example, residences are concentrated within a narrow peninsula, amid small supplementary taro and sweet potato gardens, fruit and nut trees, and small coconut plantations. Most gardens are within a twenty- to forty-minute walk from the village, although some fairly extensive gardens on steeper hillsides are one and a half to two hours' walk away. Families generally build rough shelters there in which they can sleep for several days while tending their gardens.

Landownership is related to the various levels of social organization—moiety, clan, subclan, and sub-subclan. Broad contiguous areas of land belonging to ebibinets of the same moiety are found throughout the Mandak areas. For example, Pinikindu peninsula is divided into Emalam land at the tip and Erangam land at the base. Other moiety areas on either side of the peninsula and inland some three to four miles from the coast are the residential and gardening lands of clans and subclans. The village is divided into a number of hamlets belonging to different clans; or several contiguous hamlets may represent different subclans of the same clan (map 3). Each hamlet contains from one to six dwellings for nuclear families or single adults, plus a men's house. When Pinikindu was more densely populated, a single hamlet might include two or three men's houses.

New Ireland villages display a variety of settlement patterns ranging from nucleated settlements, called "camps," to combinations of camps and hamlets. "Camp" is a local term referring to the compact settlements the Australians required New Irelanders to maintain from 1948 to 1963. Many families kept two houses, one in camp and another on their own hamlet grounds. Along the east coast today, such villages as Sominim and Lawatbura, settled by former inland peoples, appear similar to the "line" villages mentioned by Oliver for the Siuai of Bougainville, with houses set in a line on each side of a central clearing.[8] Other villages, such as Lamusong and Lambuso, reflect both patterns, with a middle core of houses lacking hamlet distinctions, surrounded on both sides by hamlet sites separated from one another by bush.

Pinikindu village is somewhat unique in its reflection of a precontact settlement form—a group of separate hamlets linked under a single village name. However, from the late 1940s to the early 1960s Pinikindu contained two areas of nucleated settlement instigated by the Australians. By 1970 one of these camps, situated near Tuwaram hamlet, had dispersed, while the main Pinikindu camp, encompassing Lekelieu, Udua, and Lewaran hamlets, had only two houses remaining which were built from camp rather than hamlet affiliations. The reason why the hamlet tradition has continued in Pinikindu may be found partly in its geography, for it includes a relatively large area off the east coast road with ample room for separate settlements. This situation contrasts with that of most east coast villages, which are cramped and compressed by the east coast road and neighboring European plantations. Another explanation has been suggested: that Pinikindu has been able to maintain its traditional settlement pattern because both moieties own lands within the peninsula.[9] Whatever the reason, the people of Pinikindu expressed a definite preference for hamlet over camp life, and during our fieldwork period they continued rebuilding old hamlets and restoring traditional men's house sites. I predict that the hamlet as a residence and social unit will be reemphasized in the near future in the Pinikindu area.

A Mandak person generally lives in two or three different hamlets during his lifetime. The predominant form of house, a rectangular structure of one or two rooms, with sago thatched roof, must be rebuilt at least every ten years. This allows people to relocate their homes in different hamlets when various social factors prod them to do so. There is no stated residence rule for a couple after marriage, although some people said that living in the wife's hamlet for one or two years after marriage was the preferred pattern. For a man, the ultimate aim is to live in his own ewentus-ebibinet hamlet, and this is almost a necessary prerequisite to attaining political power.

Residence and gardening lands are owned by clans and sub-clans, but a person has access to a variety of clan-owned plots through paternal, affinal, and other social ties. I will discuss these various avenues for gardening rights later.

POLITICAL ORGANIZATION

The Mandak reflect a common Melanesian political pattern, lacking leadership roles defined by explicit power and responsibilities. The village does not constitute a political unit in the sense of having a central authority or specific governing body. Mandak leadership is informal, and varying degrees of political power can be attained by men of recognized wealth and prestige. A number of terms are used to describe and address men of influence. *Emasa* denotes a man with the greatest recognized power and respect. There can be any number of emasas in a village. This category involves only older men over about forty-five who control an appreciable amount of wealth. Although people indicated contemporary men who would qualify as emasas, the term is no longer used. Behavior associated with an emasa is absent now, people say, for traditionally such a man would receive deferential treatment: children would not play or talk loudly in his presence, and no one walked behind him, which showed that he was not a likely victim of sorcery. People listened to an emasa and asked his advice on all manner of affairs. He would be given special treatment at feasts, be served first, and be given the best pieces of pork. Others would carry his basket home after a feast, for his hands would be too full of pork grease for him to carry it himself. Eating pork grease is associated with male strength and power. An emasa's wealth, in shell valuables and pigs, would be used in giving feasts, especially widely attended death feasts for his deceased clan members.

Erandi wuruk ("big man") and *erandi orong* ("big man") are terms still used to refer to men of influence. Erandi wuruk also may refer simply to an older man, and the term *evene wuruk* ("big woman") may refer to an older woman, both terms connoting the respect and privilege associated with old age. The "orong" adjective, which can also be used for women, connotes wealth and some degree of power, but less than that associated with an emasa. Today, erandi wuruk may indicate a man of power and prestige in the village or it may simply refer to an older man, even a "rubbish man.'' Data suggest that in the past there were more recognized status differences among men than there are today, with certain material and behavioral attributes the exclusive prerogatives of an emasa.

What are the present prerequisites for obtaining political influence among the Mandak? Criteria involve age and sex: those with political power must be males, usually past their mid-forties. Wealth and its manipulation are important: a man who wants influence must use his wealth to give feasts and activate reciprocal interactions. Wealth should not be spent for a Big Man's personal display, such as building large houses or accumulating Western products. This deliberate refraining from ostentation is also due, men indicated, to fear of envious sorcerers.

It is generally necessary for a Big Man to live in his own ewentus hamlet and to "boss" a men's house in order to direct and plan the prestige-awarding death feasts for ebibinet members buried within hamlet grounds. A helpful adjunct for political power is knowledge of magic, for use in sorcery or revenge against sorcery, taro gardening, bringing rain or sun, fishing, and healing. Taro and rain magic are among the more important skills of a Big Man, since they can be used to increase wealth and are important features of the feasting complex. A large ebibinet or ewentus is not a prerequisite for attaining power. For example, the two most influential men in Pinikindu in 1970 were members of small and dying ebibinets. A variety of extraclan ties can be used to engender a following so that a man need not depend solely on his own clan for political support.

No special term is used for the man who bosses a social unit. The men recognized for making decisions concerning ebibinet or ewentus affairs are its older members. They usually live in the ewentus's hamlet and are in charge of its men's house. When asked the leader of a particular social unit, people give the name of its oldest male. Such a person may be a kind of honorary leader, since a few men so named were invalids, blind, crippled, and senile, with no real power. The oldest active male is the one who actually makes the decisions, but deference is always given to the most ancient representative of the social unit.

Western-introduced positions of leadership are less important to attaining actual influence than are the traditional avenues and criteria for power. While all recognized Big Men in 1970 had at one time assumed a Western leadership position, *luluai*, *tultul*, or more recently komiti or councillor, these roles do not guarantee true political power and influence over decisions affecting groups larger than a hamlet. A number of former tultuls and luluais could not be described as Big Men with recognized power, and the komiti and councillor roles are often assumed by young men in their twenties and thirties, an age which has not yet attained a knowledge worthy of deference.

ALIEN INFLUENCES

Within Papua New Guinea, the people of New Ireland are among those with the most protracted contact with Western and Asian (Chinese and Japanese) sociocultural elements. Europeans possibly made their presence known to New Irelanders as early as the sixteenth century in the voyages of Portuguese and Spanish explorers, and during the seventeenth and eighteenth centuries the island was visited by Dutch, English, and French explorers. There are local stories of "blackbirding" from the Mandak area in pre-German days, probably by English ships looking for plantation workers for Samoa, Fiji, or Australia. Intensive Western contact did not begin until the late nineteenth century when the Germans and English became interested in trading and plantations. The first plantations on New Ireland were established by the Germans in the 1880s, and in 1884 Germany claimed New Ireland, called Neu Mecklenburg, as part of its Pacific territory. Kavieng was established in 1900 and Namatanai in 1904 as centers for pacifying the local peoples. The European plantation economy grew steadily from the late nineteenth century until World War I, and extensive coastal areas were planted for the copra market on lands taken from local peoples with minimal recompense. The luluai-tultul system of indirect rule was instituted in the early 1900s, during the German period of colonial rule. The east coast road from Kavieng to Namatanai was built by conscripted local labor under the direction of the German administrator Buluminski.

With the outbreak of World War I in 1914, Australia took over the German areas of New Guinea, including Neu Mecklenburg, which was renamed New Ireland. From 1921 to 1942 New Ireland was administered by Australia as part of a Mandate from the League of Nations. In 1942, Japanese forces invaded and occupied New Ireland until Australia again took over in 1945. In the process of reorganization of the League of Nations, New Ireland became in 1949 part of the Territory of Papua and New Guinea, which was to be administered by Australia under the United Nations. In December

1973 the territory, henceforth called Papua New Guinea, was granted self-government, and it achieved complete independence in the fall of 1975.

Among the most influential alien forces in New Ireland have been the Christian missions. Methodist missions established themselves in central New Ireland in the late nineteenth century; a Methodist mission was first built in Pinikindu in 1905. Roman Catholics set up missions in the Mandak area about a decade later. Until after World War II, much of the Western medical and educational contact was through schools and medical posts maintained by the two religious groups.

Today, Catholicism and Methodism (United Church) appear to be fairly equally divided in adherents among the Mandak. Lamusong is the center for a large Catholic church staffed by a resident American priest and for a church-supported primary school. Local New Irelanders preside over churches in other Mandak villages. At Kimidan an Australian priest directs a United Church mission, which includes a church, a primary school, and a small maternity hospital administered by an Australian nurse. Two Australian Seventh-Day Adventists occasionally lived in one Pinikindu hamlet in 1970, but they were able to make only one convert in the village.

Another sign of Western influence in the Mandak area is the recently built concrete block council house at Konos, which is used for meetings of the Central New Ireland District Council, established in 1962, and for other political functions. The local police station, district court, and residences for Australian patrol officers are located in a complex adjoining Konos village. A United Church primary school, taught by a local New Irelander, adjoins Pinikindu village. Mandak children attend secondary schools in the northern villages of Utu, Madina, Mongop, and the southern village of Lemeris. A government-maintained aid post attended by a local medical man is situated at Kapidan between the villages of Pinikindu and Sominim.

Other Western elements in the Mandak region are the Australian plantations. A coconut plantation owned and managed by Australians adjoins Pinikindu lands to the south, but contact between villagers and plantation managers is minimal. Occasionally a Mandak man will work a term as labor overseer on a nearby plantation, and women will be hired by the half-day to prepare copra. Although there is some interaction between the Mandak and New Guinea workers hired by the Australians, most of the Mandak have little contact with the plantation society.

In the period between World War II and the late 1950s, and to a lesser extent from the late 1930s to 1945, it was not uncommon for Mandak men to work for one to three years for Europeans. Many went to work as unskilled laborers in the New Guinea gold fields, or in Rabaul, or on local Australian- or German-owned plantations. This pattern no longer exists, for today young men who emigrate temporarily or permanently generally go as teachers, semiskilled workers, or soldiers.

Asian influences in New Ireland in the historical past have been predominately Chinese. Although the Japanese controlled the island during World War II, their occupation had little effect on Mandak culture, for it was mainly a disruptive period, with the Mandak fleeing into the interior to avoid Japanese labor conscription. The Chinese have been in New Ireland since the early 1900s. They live almost entirely in the settlements of Kavieng and Namatanai. In 1969 the Chinese constituted most of the reported 235 persons of Asian and mixed races in Kavieng. Their main livelihood is in trading and retailing. For most of the Mandak, interaction with the Chinese has been limited, as customers in small trade stores. Some of the Chinese also serve as intermediaries in the buying and selling of copra and cocoa.

In conclusion, the Mandak have been in contact with various elements of Western European and Asian society for more than eighty years. In 1970–71, my general impression was that a certain degree of stability had been reached in intercultural relationships in central New Ireland. In their daily lives, the Mandak's contacts with foreigners are mainly with representatives of the Catholic or Methodist churches, Australian nurses and teachers, Chinese or Australian store clerks in Kavieng, and government officials at Konos. For most, these contacts are sporadic and infrequent since more and more religious, medical, educational, and political matters are being managed locally by New Irelanders. A kind of stability has been reached in the kind and quantity of Western and Asian products used in the local villages. Except for major items such as trucks and radios, which are difficult to obtain and have a short life span because repair services are not accessible, most households own the same type and quantity of store-bought goods and are able to replenish their small supplies without economic stress. The Mandak show indications of slowly increasing wealth, in Australian terms, and a developing ability to direct some of the Western-introduced forms of socioeconomic organization. At the same time, traditional features of the Mandak world reflect Western contacts but also are continuing along their own paths of development—toward elaboration or decline.

2   Nurture

A FOCAL SYMBOL

The focal symbol of Mandak social distinctions will be called "nurture." The meaning of nurture lies in a complex metaphor associating the initiation (procreation), growth, and continuation of the person and social unit with the giving and receiving of nourishment, wealth, labor, and all things which sustain person and social unit. Social relationships revolve around the giving and receiving of nurture, which represents the most encompassing, most inclusive of Mandak social symbolizations. Nurture demarcates the human from the nonhuman social world and separates spheres of supportive social interactions from inimicial ones. I selected this term for the Mandak focal symbol because of the word's signification as that which nourishes, sustains, and supports the development of someone or something. Sharing and exchanging food are central Mandak idioms used in many contexts to create and communicate the social relationships of nurture. However, it is equally important to remember that the focal symbol also encompasses the giving and receiving of anything which contributes to growth and continuation of the person and social unit—for example, magic, land, labor, skills, or wealth.

The full meaning of the Mandak verb -*vasik* expresses the essence of nurture. While -vasik may be translated simply as "to procreate," its cultural meaning is immensely more complex. This complexity is actually nothing more than the term's signification as a symbol interrelated with other linked or contrasting associations, but such meaning is often denied to other peoples' concepts. -Vasik cannot be reduced to a "kinship" linkage, the means for forming consanguineal bonds. A translation of this verb as "to procreate" simply indicates "initiatory" relationships and must not be confused with American symbolizations about procreation.

The Mandak express with a single verb, -vasik, both male and female procreative roles. In Neo-Melanesian, -vasik is glossed as *karim*, "to give birth, to be pregnant." I was confused, therefore, when I first heard a man use himself as the subject of -vasik, along with his Neo-Melanesian translation, "mi karim pikinini." When asked for an explanation, he replied that although a man does not physically "give birth," yet one can say he does because the father as well as the mother contributes to a child's procreation.

Mandak concepts of procreation contrast with the biogenetic processes of American kinship concepts.[1] In initiating and developing the fetus, and later the infant, providing sustenance for the child is regarded by the Mandak as of primary significance for the ensuing social relationships. A person is born and "grown" through prestations of nurture. It is not only at the person-to-person level that this focal symbol encompasses life-supporting relationships, but also at the level of the social unit. Nurture is expressed through the growth, continuation, and interrelationships of clans and subclans. The same symbolic process of procreation which produces the individual also creates social units—both exist within and through nurturing interrelationships.

While nurture is a generalized metaphor encompassing the supportive side of social life, the Mandak world also includes antisocial individual intentions and actions. The Mandak say that death in their society comes too early for most—a result of uncontrolled angry passions among persons who work one another's destruction through secret acts of sorcery. It is not so among all peoples, for whereas in other societies people die of old age, "when their work is finished," among the Mandak people too often fall victim to capricious sorcery. While the sorcerer and his victim are not expected to share "close" nurturing relationships, even supposedly strong bonds of nurture may be subverted by a sorcerer's desire to belie general suspicions of his previous death-dealing acts. In the face of these unpredictable individual antisocial motivations, the Mandak continue to support life with countermeasures of nurturing.

Whereas death is often sudden and unpredictable, the continuation of life cannot be worked out quickly, for it depends on deliberate, ongoing nurturing interactions among persons. Nurture opposes death not only in its ends but also in its processual means. In contrast to the nearby Duke of Yorks,[2] the Mandak do not appear to be candidates for a cargo cult based on quick results, for their social experience is directed toward continuous, deliberate proceedings in human relationships. Worthwhile things, the Mandak say, are not accomplished quickly, but develop gradually out of slowly prepared, reiterated intentions. As will be discussed later, the way a person effects a change in clan membership involves reiterating certain symbolic expressions over many years. The establishment of a new hamlet or the renovation of an old one does not result in the immediate construction of a new men's house. Although the latter is an extremely important feature in Mandak social life, a men's house must be built by residents who have demonstrated their hamlet affiliations for five to ten years. I was continually impressed by Mandak explanations of the care and time with which valued things should be effected and with their emphasis on a foundation of demonstrated social relationships as the basis for new symbolic statements—whether a new men's house, a change in clan membership, or the recognition of a new relationship. Thus at our "going away" feast, a Pinikundu Big Man made a speech in which he said that the feast was not on such a grand scale as the Notsi feast given a month previously for departing anthropologist Phillip Lewis, because, he said, whereas Lewis had completed his second fieldwork residence among the Notsi, we were just finishing our first. When we left a second time, he continued, the Mandak would give us a departure feast like Lewis's. This expression of demonstrated effort and development in social relationships is very much an aspect of the focal symbol of nurture. Life is maintained through the slow succoring of the fetus, infant, person, and social unit within a network of nurturing interrelationships.

While the focal symbol incorporates the generalized terms in which the Mandak constitute their social relationships, nurture is not expressed explicitly as a focal symbol in many contexts. Nurture is created implicitly in multiple contexts through differentiating expressions—through the forms, therefore, of maternal nurture, paternal substance, and affinal nurture. It is because of this pattern of articulation that a summation of the signification of the focal symbol is not possible except by explicating the major symbols and their interrelationships. For the most part, nurture incorporates the "similarities" within which the differentiating symbols exist and against which they are expressed. The "landscape" of nurture is formed by the symbolic distinctions which I now introduce; the encompassing aspects of nurture are the implicitly created background against which certain symbolic features are differentiated. In this discussion, therefore, I have but briefly touched on the meaning of nurture; its full significance will emerge gradually throughout the book.

Maternal Nurture

Introduction

Although both male and female provide nurture, their contributions form culturally significant differentiations synthesized in symbolizations which I interpret as "maternal nurture" and "paternal substance." These oppositional and complementary symbolizations are expressed in the context of Mandak concepts about procreation. A person is conceived in the *ebolout* ("womb") of its mother. Through several acts of intercourse, the male progenitor projects semen into the female's womb to form the substance of the fetus. While the semen is said to unite with an egg in the womb, it is the male-given substance alone which contributes the blood, skin, and internal organs of the fetus. The female's role is to nourish and protect the male-provided substance, and throughout gestation the infant is fed in the womb entirely from maternal sources. The father does not "feed" the fetus through intercourse during gestation as some Melanesian people believe. Among the Mandak, as soon as a woman knows she is pregnant she should not have intercourse for the remainder of her pregnancy and the ensuing one and a half to two years of nursing. To do so would endanger the life of the fetus/infant, although the exact nature of this danger was not fully clarified.

While -vasik, associating both paternal and maternal procreative roles, serves as a metaphor of cognatic relationships, further symbolizations differentiate the way the sexes provide nurture. A person's primary and essential sustenance is derived from female procreative functions. It is because of this, the Mandak say, that they follow their mothers rather than their fathers in ebibinet and ewentus membership. Social-unit identification and definition are expressed, therefore, through maternal nurture expressions. I have chosen the term "maternal nurture" because these symbolic expressions emphasize the provision of sustenance and support associated with female procreation. Although a more complete meaning of maternal nurture will be explicated throughout this study, at this point it is enough to say that the symbol communicates one kind of social definition in Mandak society, an identity of people *within* social units rather than *across* unit boundaries.

Idioms of Maternal Nurture

Some frequently used idioms of the maternal nurture symbolization include the following.

Ebolout ("Womb")

Ebolout is the first nurturing environment of the Mandak person—the maternal womb in which he was protected and fed until birth. The idiom conveys a social unit solidarity of particularly strong moral force. Persons who link themselves through references to a common womb emphasize the strength of the maternal nurture bond between them. It is the sibling relationship (*metak* or *minmin*) which is usually recalled through forms of this symbolic idiom—a sibling bond within one of the smallest social units, the subclan or sub-subclan. When a person wants to emphasize social solidarity with another in the metak or minmin relationship within his own ewentus he may say: "we are of one womb." This is not a literal expression meaning that they have the same biological mother but communicates a kind of social identity between the persons so linked—a social identity of shared maternal nurture. The exact nature of the moral force conjoining two or more persons "of one womb" will be considered in discussions of the metak and minmin categories in chapter 3.

It is interesting that the Mandak word for their traditional "oven," a mound of heated stones which covers and bakes food, is *ebolowat*. Since the term for "stone" is *ewat*, it appears that "stone oven" may involve a conjunction of ebolout and ewat. If this is so, the etiology of ebolowat is appropriate to the suggested symbolic association between social unit membership and female nurture. The stone oven is where most Mandak food is cooked and is the source, therefore, of "food sustenance," just as the womb is the initial locus of a person's maternal nurture, a symbol of social unit membership. Another extension of the ebolout idiom will be mentioned in later discussions of the men's house, the eantuing.

Erus "Breast, Breast Milk"

Erus is another symbolic idiom which appears in expressions of solidarity within the ewentus, subclan, or sub-subclan. In contrast to ebolout, however, erus links individuals not only in sibling categories, but in other maternal nurture relationships as well. Like ebolout, erus suggests a strong moral force of shared social unit obligations and identity.

The erus idiom recalls the mother's provision of sustenance for the infant through nursing. To emphasize relationship between people of the same clan subdivision, the Mandak will say, "they come from one breast." This does not refer to a consanguineal connection but is a metaphorical expression of maternal nurture bonds. To say that two men came from the same breast does not mean that an actual genealogical link can be traced to one woman who nursed them or even to an ancestral grandmother; rather, it expresses a kind of moral obligation between them.

The Mandak word ewentus suggests a conjunction between *evene* ("woman") and erus. For example, "boy drinks milk" is *emandak i tus*. Thus the Mandak term for subclan and sub-subclan appears to reiterate a symbolic idiom used to communicate the kind of relationship encompassed by these social units.

In Neo-Melanesian, ewentus is translated as *susu*, which is also used to translate erus. Susu may serve simply as a gloss for ewentus: for example, *dispela man, em i bilong wanem susu*? ("This man, he belongs to what ewentus?") It is also used as a symbolic idiom: for example, *mipela bilong wanpela susu tasol* ("we all belong to one breast only").

Sharing Food

The larger social units of ebibinet and moiety are associated with a symbolic idiom of "sharing food." This idiom is expressed as: "sharing food," "eating together," and "giving food." An important aspect of "sharing food" is that people give and receive nourishment without paying or expecting payment. Just as the individual does not pay for sustenance received from his mother's womb and breast, so also those enjoined by sharing food do not make exchanges for extended nurture. Members of the same social unit, whether ewentus, ebibinet, or moiety, are those who are related through references to sharing food.

It is appropriate to Mandak social ideology that references to sharing food recall relationships within larger social units, while the more physiologically oriented idioms, ebolout and erus, refer to ties within the ewentus. Actual genealogical connections are generally neither known nor emphasized between people of the same ebibinet or moiety, nor are subclans of the same ebibinet tied in a genea-logical framework. It is only within the smallest unit, sub-subclan, that actual procreative relationships can be stated upon request.

Female Nurture

evene ilogi ebibinet

"woman is the clan"

The above metaphor is a shared Mandak expression which communicates the maternal nurture symbol. "Female" is a most important idiom of maternal nurture, although the symbol is used to relate both sexes. The idioms erus and ebolout refer to female body parts and functions involved with gestation and parturition. At the ebibinet level, the reference to sharing food is also a female idiom, as emphasized in symbolic associations between female, taro, and social unit. Taro is the major Mandak "cultural" food, necessary to all feasting occasions and a vital part of most rituals and cere-monies. This plant is said to have been given to the Mandak by a culture heroine, Sigidigum, and has always belonged to the women's sphere of labor and knowledge. The names of taro varieties may be taken as personal names only by females.

Although I did not have the opportunity to pursue taro classifi-cation, five or six women gave me the names of sixty taro varieties grown by the Mandak, and I was assured that other women must know forty to fifty more. Some of these varieties belong to particular clans, and it was suggested that most taro types might once have been the property of different social units. Ebibinet ownership of a taro variety grants its owners the exclusive right to distribute the plant's cuttings to those outside the ebibinet at feasts or in various exchanges: these cuttings may then be planted in the recipients' gardens.

A "firstfruits" feast, *eankonkomun* (*ean-*, "to eat," *-konko-*, "the start of," *-mun*, "food") reiterates the taro/social unit asso-ciation. When a new garden is cultivated on fallow land, the first taro harvested is brought to the men's house of the landowning ewentus. Because of the variety of land-use patterns, the person cultivating the garden may or may not be a member of this social unit, but the first taro crop must come back to the subclan from whose land it gained its sustenance. No feasts are held to mark the initial harvest of other plants.

The Mandak person begins and ends his life in association with taro. It is the first food given to a newborn infant after mother's milk. When a woman senses that birth is imminent, she should begin cooking a type of "soft" taro. After the delivery, when the infant has been washed and nursed, a *nanga* (M, MZ, etc.) should feed the baby a small portion of masticated taro. Without this early introduction to the tuber, a baby may later sicken and die, although I did not learn the exact reason for this danger. In the past a person ideally also ended his life in association with taro. When an individual died of old age, the corpse was propped up in a specially prepared chair and surrounded by mounds of taro which were said to be for the spirit of the deceased and were not eaten by people at the burial feast.

A Mandak Metaphor

The metaphor *evene ilogi ebibinet* ("woman is the clan") is a shared Mandak expression. The creation of cultural meaning through metaphorical connections is not static but is a continuing dialogue involving both reaffirmation and innovation. I gained much insight when knowledgeable persons created new metaphors to explain to me various aspects of their social ideology.

In discussing Mandak concepts about the ebibinet, a particularly insightful man defined it in the following terms. In reply to my question, "What is the ebibinet?", he said: "The ebibinet is closed, fastened, it is something which doesn't have holes, it cannot be broken. It is closed altogether." With his hands he made the image of a watertight container. The metaphor this man used reiterates aspects of the maternal nurture symbol. The "watertight container" image recalls the ebolout (womb), the first container in which the Mandak finds nurture. The metaphor expresses the idea that the ebibinet surrounds, protects, and nourishes its enclosed members. Its boundaries are firm and unambiguous. The ebibinet may be visualized as a projection at the level of social unit of the nurturing environment between procreating mother and her child.

Symbols of Identity

While the sharing of maternal nurture distinguishes and expresses relationships within social units, certain other symbolizations display a different function in social differentiation. These symbolizations, which I interpret as "symbols of identity," are used to particularize, in time and place, social units of the same scale. I will discuss these symbols as they are used to identify and distinguish particular moieties, clans, and subclans.

Moiety: Emalam and Erangam

While the moieties, Emalam and Erangam, are in anthropological terms matrilineal, the basis for membership is explained differently by the Mandak. Criteria for inclusion in a moiety are not expressed in the same way as those for inclusion in an ebibinet or an ewentus. The Mandak describe their dual organization in the following terms. In the beginning, when human societies were first established, all peoples were divided into two contrasting types which were recognized by the Mandak as Emalam and Erangam. The world of humans is so divided, although not every society organizes this duality for social purposes. The Mandak say that moiety membership is established before birth by unknown forces, just as people do not know how the sex of the fetus is determined. Each person is born a member of one of these two divisions, and the diversity shows in certain physical traits. For example, those who are Emalam have four lines on the palms of their hands, those who are Erangam have only three. Emalam people walk leading with their left foot, Erangam with the right. One Pinikindu man said that when he was working in Rabaul he could tell whether a European was Emalam or Erangam by watching the way he walked down the street. Although people also stated that a person receives his moiety name from his mother, no one would suggest or support the idea that a person derives from her the physical traits of moiety membership. Although the Mandak recognize the link between mother-child and moiety membership, they conceptualize their dual division as an innate feature of human beings. I will return to this contrast between moiety and ebibinet-ewentus membership in the latter part of this book.

When the human duality was first established, each ebibinet was assigned to one of the two divisions and the Mandak custom of marrying out of one's moiety began. No genealogical connections are suggested between ebibinets of the same moiety.

The symbols of identity which differentiate the moieties are the names of the moiety eagles, Emalam and Erangam. The first is larger, a variety of sea eagle (*Haliaetus leucogaster*) with white-tipped black wings and a white head. Emalam lives off both sea and bush life, fish and snakes. Erangam (*Pandion leucocephalus*), a smaller variety of sea hawk with similar markings, feeds entirely on sea life. Neither bird should be killed or eaten. No origin myths were found connecting the moieties to their namebirds. Various forms of magic are connected with both birds; a particularly strong type used to revenge sorcery deaths is associated with the Emalam bird, while a much less important form—used to cause headaches—is associated with Erangam. However, any man of either moiety may possess one or both forms of magic.

Ebibinet

A symbol of identity which distinguishes between and within clans is the *erunda*, a nonhuman, localized spirit associated with each ebibinet. The erunda may take the form of a snake, turtle, fish, pig, or other animal, or it may dwell disembodied in some natural feature such as a rock or a pool of water. Each ebibinet is identified with from one to four of these nonhuman spirits. An erunda is dangerous to humans and can cause injury or death to those who venture close to its habitat. Although ebibinet members are in less danger from their own erunda, no one takes proximity to it lightly. Affines have no protection from each other's erundas. For example, a man would not go near the erunda of his son's ebibinet, nor a woman near her husband's erunda.

The erunda is a symbol of ebibinet identity. For example, in explaining the relationship between two persons of different subclans of the same clan, people may say: "They belong to Kasasambwang and Tawapa (ewentuses) but they share one erunda." One man defined erunda as the name which comes and "fastens together" all subclans of one ebibinet.

Historical relationships of particular persons and subdivisions within a clan may be expressed by reference to associations with these nonhuman spirits. After the prerequisite exchanges are performed, a small ebibinet may become part of another ebibinet of the same moiety. To indicate, when circumstances demand, that certain individuals are relatively new members of a clan, people will say: "Yes, this man belongs to Kaluan ebibinet, but he has a different erunda [than 'true' Kaluan members]." Although I found no historical data to support or refute the idea, the origin of multiple nonhuman spirits associated with one social unit may derive from a former merging of separate ebibinets.

The locality of the erunda is also used to support historical claims to ebibinet land. Clans which have recently been given land in a new area do not have a resident erunda. I found no evidence on whether through time an erunda can change its homesite. However, one particularly ambitious Big Man in Pinikindu, a second-generation new member of Kaluan clan, has asserted that his erunda, a fish, traditionally situated to the south near his grandmother's clan land, is gradually moving up the coast to his present Kaluan hamlet.

Ewentus

The identity symbol of the ewentus, a subclan or sub-subclan, is its *eantuing*, a men's house with an enclosed yard. Since I discuss the eantuing in detail in chapter 4, I will merely point out here that people identify their affiliation with a particular ewentus by reference to a specific eantuing. It is within the men's-house yard that all ewentus members, male and female, are buried, and within the ewentus's eantuing that death feasts for subclan members are planned and in part carried out. An ewentus and its eantuing generally share the same name, although owing to the beginnings or demise of a subclan from resettlement or death of all its members there are also numerous cases in which the ewentus and its eantuing have different names. For example, members of Tawapa ewentus have been residing for the past thirty years at Udua hamlet. This hamlet formerly belonged to another clan, but the owning clan gradually died out and Tawapa residents established rights to Udua by contributing to the death feasts of the declining ebibinet. At the same time, Tawapa people at Udua gradually sold out rights to their own hamlet, known as Tawapa. In such a case there has been a lag in eantuing-ewentus name association which will probably continue for the present generation. For example, Ligidak, a man belonging to Tawapa ewentus, referred to the Tawapa eantuing as his "true" eantuing and to the name Tawapa as his subclan. He also identified himself as a man of Udua, as his social unit name, and as a place where the Tawapa people are recently being buried.

Symbols of identity differentiate particular social units from other units of the same scale. These symbols contrast in function with those which may collectivize moral behavior without reference to historical identities. When people communicate relationships to one another through the idioms of ebolout, erus, or sharing food, they indicate varying degrees of moral force in regard to the kind of behavior encompassed by the maternal nurture metaphor. In contrast, when people refer to relationships through the symbols of identity, they point to historical, particularizing differentiations and solidarities. Such symbols do not appear to be interrelated in a "logical" pattern: that is, the meaning of the moiety symbols, Emalam and Erangam, is not incomplete without the ebibinet's erunda symbols. However, the symbols of nurture, maternal nurture, paternal substance, and affinal nurture cannot be understood except in their interrelationships with one another. Symbols of identity also include, for example, personal names. Such symbols are particularizing rather than generalizing in that while they collectivize individuals into groups, they are used to differentiate one person or group from another of the same order. Thus when a man speaks of sharing one womb with another person, he recalls the meaning of a certain category and thus generalizes the situation. In contrast, when a man refers to himself as belonging to Emalam or Tawapa (an ewentus-eantuing), or as associated with a certain erunda, he identifies himself among others in a mesh of particular moieties, clans, and subclans. Reference to such symbols, therefore, localizes a person within a group of historically specific, named groups.

Summary

While three or four different levels of social unit, from moiety to sub-subclan, are encompassed by the maternal nurture symbol, they are *all one kind of category*. This symbol indicates that those connected in such relationships share rather than exchange nurture. Maternal nurture bonds also separate the sexes in that sexual intercourse, procreation, and marriage are forbidden between those conjoined by the symbolization. Maternal nurture refers to relationships that are conceptually female and stand in opposition to those which are male. This metaphor generalizes symbolic expresssions of female nurture, as an association of incorporation and continuation in Mandak social relationships.

Paternal Substance

In Mandak procreation ideology, the male progenitor provides the blood, bone, and internal organs of the fetus which is fed in its mother's womb. The male procreative role involves a prestation—a gift of substance to his offspring. The Mandak say that the male "makes the child come up .... stand up." The symbolic idiom most commonly used to convey the meaning of paternal substance is "blood." Western ideas of kinship must not be confused with this consanguineal reference, for when the Mandak speak of blood relationships they are conveying something quite different from the American meaning of the term.

The symbol which both complements and opposes maternal nurture and which relates a person to male procreative nurture I call "paternal substance." This term was selected because of the primacy of blood as a frequently used symbolic idiom recalling the complex meaning of this symbolization. In contrast to maternal nurture, which defines social unit membership, paternal substance identifies a person with cross-unit relationships. Commonly used idioms of the symbol include: *enda* or *enat* ("blood"), and *-lok* ("to make come up, to bring about"). Such idioms are used not in simple statements relating father to offspring, but rather in symbolic expressions recalling moral expectations which oppose and complement those evoked by maternal nurture. For example, I heard the term "blood" applied to the relationship between a woman and the ebibinet of a man who had recently married her divorced, elderly mother. The woman did not derive literally from the substance of her stepfather, but in this particular circumstance she was involved in an event which was typical of normative relationships between persons related through paternal substance.

While maternal nurture partakes of the female side of the sexual dichotomy, paternal substance provides the male complement. Thus an association of male, exchanging, and cross-unit relationships opposes the maternal nurture elements of female, sharing, and same-unit relationships. Idioms of paternal substance focus on male prestations of substance at procreation, while maternal nurture idioms emphasize the continual provision of sustenance by females. The former is concerned with relationships which are *other* than oneself and outside ego's social unit; the latter marks social ties which are of the *same kind* as oneself and within ego's social unit.

Paternal substance is a distinction of the focal symbol of nurture and is expressed in relationships which entail the prestation of food, wealth, labor, knowledge, and all else included as nurture. However, paternal substance bonds also contrast with those of maternal nurture and evoke a different kind of response. The nurture a person receives outside the boundaries of his maternal nurture unit must eventually be paid off, exchanged against. The extension of paternal substance, a cross-unit kind of nurture, makes the recipient's ewentus indebted to the blood ewentus.

Thus far I have been speaking of cross-unit relationships generally without specifying the particular level of unit interaction. Maternal nurture idioms are used to refer varyingly to moiety, clan, subclan, and sub-subclan levels. Paternal substance idioms are similar, although their expressions tend to evoke a narrower range of moral force, mainly between two intermarrying subclans, and to a lesser extent between ebibinets. In a few contexts, discussed later, paternal substance symbols are applied to intermoiety interactions. Since marriage and procreation are prohibited within the moiety, units inside Erangam and Emalam are never joined or related by paternal substance.

Conclusion

Major social distinctions of the Mandak are interpreted in this study through four interrelated symbols: nurture, maternal nurture, paternal substance, and affinal nurture. The focal symbol, nurture, is expressed particularly in the signification of -vasik, to procreate. People are related in different ways through the kinds of nurture they give and receive. Nurture as female procreation entails the sharing of food and wealth within social units, while it excludes marriage, sexual relations, and further procreation within these units. Maternal nurture thus binds persons together into joint nurturing groups which cannot, however, initiate their own perpetuation. The major idioms used to express this symbol are: ebolout ("womb"), erus ("breast, breast milk"), and sharing food.

Nurture as male procreation involves a contrasting but complementary symbol. The main idioms of this symbol, paternal substance, are enat, enda ("blood") and "to make come up," "to make stand up." In contrast to female nurture, which provides continuity, paternal substance initiates social units and persons through prestations of substance—nurture. In paternal substance relationships, nurture is extended across maternal nurture boundaries and elicits exchanges rather than continual sharing.

Bonds of procreative nurture exclude sexual intercourse and marriage within certain prescribed social unit boundaries. Maternal nurture excludes sexual intercourse and marriage altogether, extending to the moiety level. Paternal substance forbids marriage and sexual relations within nurture bonds of strong moral force, between ego and the subclans of his or her father and mother's father. In a third symbolization of nurture, which crosses unit boundaries through marriage, food and wealth are given and received between spouses and their respective social units. I refer to this symbolization as affinal nurture, and it also elicits cross-unit exchanging. Affinal nurture is discussed in chapter 4 in connection with further consideration of the sexual dichotomy in Mandak social differentiations.

3   Small Callings

Social Categories

The Mandak address and refer to one another through
a set of interrelated social categories which in behavioral norms
contrast with and complement one another to express the major
tenets of shared social symbolizations. Although these categories
coexist with status distinctions of age, sex, political power, and skill,
they do not contrast with other kinds of relationships. As one man
replied when I was probing for a Mandak word meaning "family" or
"kin": "No, we have no words like that, only many small callings,
like *tamak* or *nanga*, which we use for everyone we know."
The social categories presented here are referred to by their
Mandak terms. These are used in both address and reference,
although the exact form of referential usage may vary according to
the grammatical structure of a sentence. The categorical terms are
the Mandak answers to the questions: "X, what is Y [personal
name] to you? What do you call Y?"
In this chapter I will discuss the Mandak social distinctions which
are shared and communicated through their "small callings." What
are the normative behavioral expectations for each social category?
What kind of interactions does a person expect of someone he calls,
for example, "*metak*," and how does he respond to this relationship? What kinds of signification do the Mandak recognize in each
social category? The "small callings" are not mere manifestations of
a set of ideal rules, but rather are themselves the shared forms of
social symbolizations—of the Mandak nurture symbols. Thus nurture, maternal nurture, paternal substance, and affinal nurture are
culturally recognized expressions which occur in the multiple contexts of social category interactions. Relationships between the
nurture symbols, the articulation of a pattern, are also the products
of interrelationships between social categories.
The Mandak defined their "small callings" for me through various
articulations of the verbs *-vasik* ("to procreate") and *-puké* ("to

marry"). It is possible, therefore, to describe the categories in terms of genealogical criteria, as presented in table 1. I ascribed genealogical relationships to each term by recording numerous individual genealogies and then asking ego: "What [category] do you call X [personal name]?" Although I present the data in table 1 for readers interested in generating such patterns, I must emphasize that genealogical definitions of Mandak categories add little if anything to comprehension of their cultural signification. A genealogical pattern can be produced by focusing on one aspect of the cultural logic of each categorical definition, but the Mandak themselves do not think in terms of genealogical frameworks. People found my recording of their genealogies quite tedious. Although each person knew exactly what he called every individual with whom he had contact, such categorical relationships often were not founded on either known or fictitious genealogical relationships. It was difficult for people to recall categories of long deceased kin or of persons several generations removed. For example, when I asked one man "What do you call your DDS?" he called over three knowledgeable elderly men to determine the answer. They debated for some time and finally agreed upon the proper response for the man who had a DDS living in New Guinea and thus a possible actual relationship should the latter ever come to New Ireland.

The criteria the Mandak use to place individuals in particular social categories are varied. A person is born into a set of nurturing relationships and begins his own social network from these and their respective nurturing interactions. Often, however, the defined cultural logic of the categorical pattern determines the choices a person may make in establishing a particular relationship with another individual. For example, when I asked a man, X, why he called a certain woman, Y, "*minmin*" (cross-sex sibling), he replied that another minmin of his had once been married to the man M. She had died about ten years ago and M had since remarried twice. His third wife, Y, is called "minmin" by X because, X said, she "replaced" his other minmin when she married M. Before her marriage, X had called her "*nanga*" (M, MZ, etc.). People often have a choice among two or more alternatives in determining a particular social category, and individuals often seem to emphasize certain relationships for political purposes.

While each social category entails a set of behavioral norms, the relative strength of such norms varies from dyad to dyad. One aspect of the anthropological dispute about the nature of "kinship"

Table 1. Mandak Social Categories

		MATERNAL NURTURE CATEGORIES	
		female	male
nanga	Male Ego	M, MZ, FBW, FFM, MMM, MMZD, MFBD, FFBSW, FMZSW, wife of pavugu, wife's pavugu, etc.	
nanga	Female Ego	M, MZ, FBW, FFM, MMM, MFBD, MMZD, FFBSW, FMZSW, wife of egohup, etc.	
tata	Male Ego	ZD, ZDDD, MZDD, MBSDD, FBDD, FZSDD, MMZDDD, MFBDDD, FMZSDD, FFBSDD, etc.	MB, ZS, ZDDS, MZDS, MBSDS, FBDS, FZSDS, MMMB, MMZS, MFBS, MMZDDS, MFBDDS, FMZSDS, FFBSDS, etc.
tata	Female Ego		MB, MMMB, MMZS, MFBS, FFMB, etc.
minmin	Male Ego	Z, ZDD, BSDD, BDSD, SDD, DSD, ZSSD, MZD, MBSD, MZDDD, MBDSD, FBD, FZSD, FZDSD, FBDDD, MMZDD, MFBDD, FFBSD, FMZSD, etc.	
minmin	Female Ego		B, MZS, MFF, MMB, FMF, FMFB, FBS, MMZDS, FFBSS, FMZSS, MBSS, FZSS, FMZS, etc.

		MATERNAL NURTURE CATEGORIES	
		female	male
metak	Male Ego	WZ, BW, BWZ, wife of metak, metak of wife, etc.	B, ZDS, BSDS, BDSS, SDS, DSS, ZSSS, MZS, MBSS, MZDDS, MBDSS, FBS, FZSS, FZDSS, FBDDS, FMF, FFMB, MMB, MFF, MMZDS, MFBDS, FMZSS, FFBSS, etc.
metak	Female Ego	Z, MZD, FBD, FMZD, MMZDD, MFBDD, FMZSD, FFBSD, FZSD, FMFZ, MBSD, HFZ, etc.	ZH, HB, husband of metak, metak of husband etc.
emandak	Female Ego		S, ZS, BSDS, SSS, DDS, ZSSS, ZDDS, FBDS, MZDS, MMZDDS, MFBDDS, FMZSDS, FFBSDS, MBSDS, FZSDS, husband of pavugu, husband's pavugu, etc.
enek	Female Ego	D, ZD, BSDD, SSD, DDD, ZSSD, ZDDD, FBDD, MZDD, MMZDDD, MFBDDD, FMZSDD, FFBSDD, MBSDD, FZSDD, husband's egohup, etc.	

		PATERNAL SUBSTANCE CATEGORIES	
emandak	Male Ego		S, BS, BSSS, BDDS, SSS, DDS, ZDSS, MZSS, MBSSS, FBSS, FZSSS, FZDDS, MMZDSS, MFBDSS, FMZSSS, FFBSSS, WZS, WMB, etc.

		PATERNAL SUBSTANCE CATEGORIES	
		female	male
enek	Male Ego	D, BD, BSSD, BDDD, SSD, DDD, ZDSD, MZSD, MBSSD, FZDDD, WZD, MMZDSD, FMZSSD, etc.	
tamak	Female Ego		F, FB, FFF, MZH, MMF, MMZDH, MFBDH, FFBS, FMZS, etc.
tamak	Male Ego		F, FB, FMMB, FFF, MZH, MMF, MMZDH, MFBDH, FFBS, FMZS, etc.
nimugu	Female Ego	FZ, FFFZ, MMFZ, BD, FZDD, MZSD, MBDD, FFBD, FMZD, MMZDSD, MFBDSD, FFBSSD, FMZSSD, MBSSD, FZSSD, FMMZDD, MMZDSD, etc.	BS, FZDS, FBSS, MZSS, MBDS, MMZDSS, MFBDSS, FFBSSS, FMZSSS, MBSSS, FZSSS, FMMZDS, etc.
nimugu	Male Ego	FZ, MMFZ, FFBD, FMZD, etc.	
pavugu	Female Ego	FZD, MBD, MZSDD, MMZSD, MFBSD, FFBDD, FMZDD, FFBSSDD, FMMZD, etc.	
pavugu	Male Ego		FMB, ZSS, MBS, FZS, MZDSS, FBDSS, MMZSS, MFBSS, FFBDS, FMZDS, MMZDDSS, MFBDDSS, FFBSDSS, FMZSDSS, FZDDS, etc.

		PATERNAL SUBSTANCE CATEGORIES	
		female	male
egohup	Female Ego		FMB, FZS, MBS, MZSDS, MMZSS, MFBSS, FFBDS, FMZDS, FFBSSDS, FMMZS, etc.
egohup	Male Ego	ZSD, MBD, MZDSD, FZD, MMZSD, MFBSD, FFBDD, FMZDD, MMZDDSD, MFBDDSD, FFBSDSD, FMZSDSD, FZDDD, etc.	

		NURTURE CATEGORIES	
		female	male
tumbugu	Female Ego	FFZ, MM, MMZ, BSD, SD, ZSD, FZDSD, FBSSD, FBDDD, MZSSD, MZDDD, MBDSD, FM, FMZ, MFM, DD, ZDD, SDD, ZSDD, FBDSD, MZDSD, FMM, FMMZDSD, FMMZ, FZDDD, FBSDD, MBDDD, DSD, ZDSD, BDD, BSSD, MFZ, etc.	FF, FFB, SS, ZSS, BSS, FZDSS, FBSSS, FBDDS, MZSSS, MZDDS, MBDSS, MF, MFB, MFMB, DS, ZDS, SDS, ZSDS, FBDSS, MZDSS, FMMZDSS, FZDDS, FBSDS, MBDDS, DSS, ZDSS, BDS, BSSS, etc.
tumbugu	Male Ego	MM, MMZ, FFZ, BSD, SD, MZSSD, FBSSD, FM, FMZ, BDD, DD, MBDD, MZSDD, FZDD, FBSDD, MFM, MFMZ, MZSSD, FMM, MFZ, etc.	FF, FFB, BSS, SS, MZSSS, FBSSS, MF, MFB, MFMB, BDS, DS, MBDS, MZSDS, FZDS, FBSDS, etc.

(continued)

AFFINAL NURTURE CATEGORIES			
		female	male
nisok	Female Ego		husband
nisok	Male Ego	wife	
inasong	Female Ego	wife of tata, tata of nisok	tata of nisok
inasong	Male Ego	wife of tata	
erulom	Female Ego		nisok of enek
erulom	Male Ego	nanga of nisok	
ermasik	Male Ego		nisok of minmin, minmin of nisok
ermasik egohup	Male Ego		nisok of egohup, egohup of nisok
nangene	Female Ego	nisok of minmin, minmin of nisok	

MATERNAL NURTURE CATEGORIES			
		female	male
naak	Female Ego	HBW, BSW , etc.	FZH, BDH , etc.
naak	Male Ego		WZH, FZH , etc.
nenak	Female Ego	HM, SW , etc.	HF , etc.
nenak	Male Ego	SW , etc.	
namuna	Male Ego		WF, DH , etc.
nalun	Female Ego	HMBW, HZSW , etc.	

categories lies in the problem of how to deal with differential strengths of norms in a single category. For example, how does one explain why a man acts in one way with one person in X category but differently with another person whom he calls by the same term? Those who predefine social categories by genealogical criteria tend to explain such differential application of norms through variations of "extension" theories. For example, Radcliffe-Brown dealt with the problem by suggesting the extension of categories from the nuclear family to other genealogical kin based on analogies to members of the primary nuclear family.[1] Some componential analysts deal with extensions as involved with genealogical distance from ego.[2] I believe that this problem is due to the invalid imposition of a neutral genealogical grid as the determinant of social categories. If such social analysis is disengaged from this mold, more meaningful explanations may be found for the phenomena of differential normative relationships encompassed within a single category. Among the Mandak, I suggest, behavioral variations toward persons whom ego classifies by the same term result from the intersection of social categories and certain aspects of social unit organization. Behavioral differences within single categories may be described in terms of the varying application of the *moral force* of symbolizations to these categories. Among the Mandak the moral force of a relationship varies according to its inclusiveness in the structural hierarchy of ewentus, ebibinet, and moiety, or the interrelationship of these—for example, ewentus to ewentus. I will illustrate the concept of moral force with two examples.

The *minmin* category emphasizes respect and avoidance between male/female siblings. When two minmins belong to the same subclan, the moral force of the relationship is strong; that is, they share strong sanctions against social-physical interaction in all contexts. However, when two persons in a minmin category belong to different clans, the moral force is weaker—there is less social pressure for them to follow the normative avoidance restrictions. Moving from ewentus to ebibinet to moiety levels, the moral force of symbolic expressions in social categories becomes progressively milder.

In the first example, I was discussing the *normative* moral force in connection with social categories—that is, that based on the conceptual relationship between symbols, categories, and social units. In actual interactions there may not be a precise "fit" between the cultural norms and social units. For example, two Pinikindu men,

Timot and Luttam, share a *tata* (MB/ZS, etc.) relationship. Although they belong to different ebibinets, the moral force of this particular tata bond is as strong as if they were members of the same ewentus. Timot and Luttam belong to ebibinets which stand in a close relationship owing to a history of warfare, adoption, and land gifts between the two social units. In 1970, when the population of both ebibinets was very low, Timot was Luttam's sole remaining elder tata. Because the ebibinets are "close" and their members few, in this particular tata relationship a closure has occurred between moral force, social unit, and social category norms. Although in normative terms the moral force of a social category is strongest at the ewentus level and weakest at the moiety level, demographic circumstances may occasion strong moral force at the ebibinet level. Throughout this study, however, I will be discussing the normative aspects of the categories rather than statistical recordings of actual cases.

In considering the cultural signification of social categories, it is important to attend to a social group's own definitions of their person-to-person relationships. In figure 1 I have diagramed relational definitions between social categories as expressed by several Mandak individuals. In this figure, *gabasik* is the third-person singular, past imperfect form of the –vasik verb, and the form used in almost all Mandak definitions of their procreative social categories. This tense of the verb carries with it a sense of continuous action rather than a single completed action. When the Mandak want to say that a particular woman gave birth, they use the past perfect of –vasik, *garavasik pom*. In defining their social categories, therefore, the Mandak indicate that procreative relationships involve continuous nurture rather than the single event of giving birth.

Figure 1 does not depict actual procreative relationships; nor does it represent a nuclear family encapsulization of kinship categories. The meaning of gabasik is much broader than the simple gloss "he or she procreated." Figure 2 is a diagram of interrelationships between categories and their expression of maternal nurture or paternal substance.

Before discussing these social categories, I will present them briefly in much the same style represented in figure 1. Ego is *emandak* (male) or *enek* (female) to the woman (*nanga*) who procreated ego. Ego is *metak* (male or female) to a same-sex person (*metak*) who was also procreated by ego's nanga. Metaks are

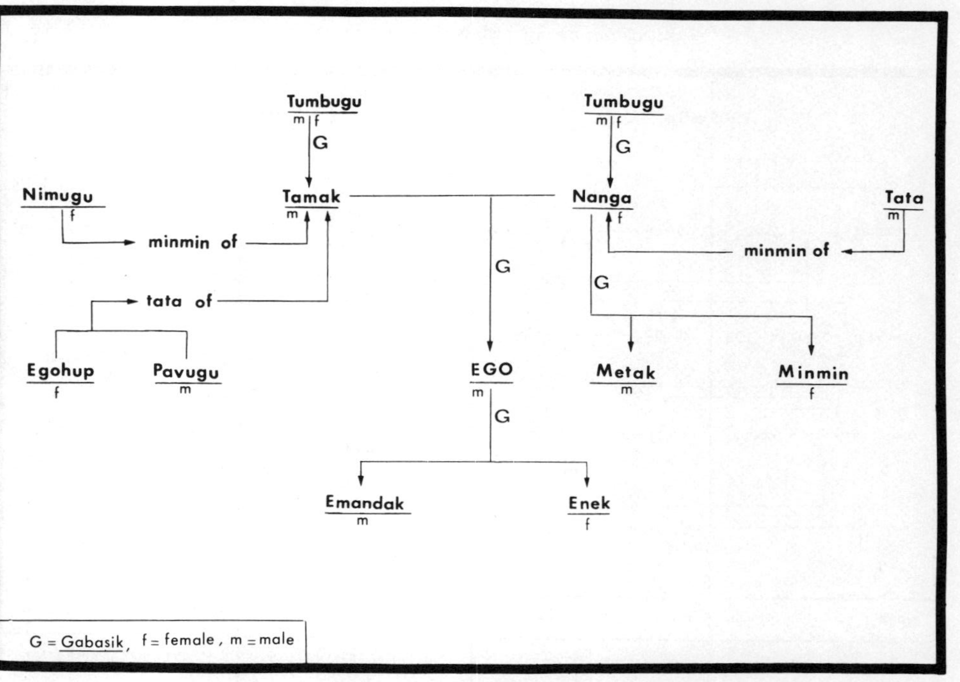

Fig. 1. Social categories from Mandak definitions

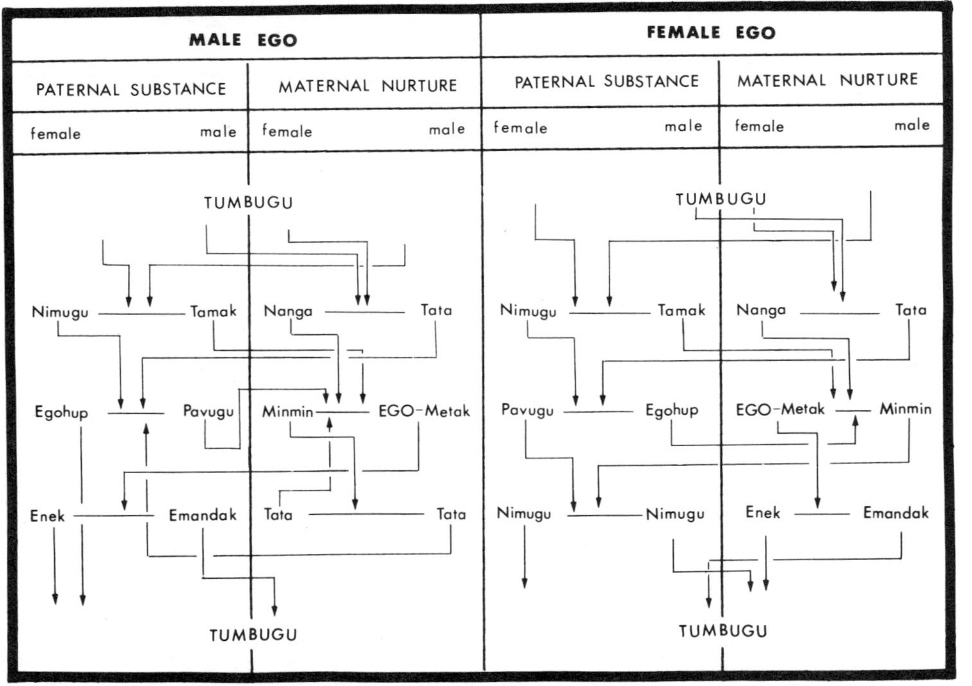

Fig. 2. Interrelationships between categories

individuals of the same sex who derive nurture from the same female source and who share within maternal nurture units, whether moiety, clan, subclan, sub-subclan, or all of these. Nanga/emandak, nanga/enek, and metak/metak are informal, cooperating, sharing relationships. Ego is *minmin* (male or female) to a person of the opposite sex (*minmin*) who was procreated by ego's nanga. This cross-sex relationship entails avoidance between male and female, who, however, share food and wealth (nurture) with one another. Ego is *tata* (male or female) to a man (*tata*) who is minmin of ego's nanga and who participates in a sharing relationship with ego.

Ego exchanges with a number of other persons in certain social categories. Ego is *emandak* (male) or *enek* (female) to the man (*tamak*) who procreated ego and who married ego's nanga. Tamak/emandak and tamak/enek are informal, cooperative relationships. Ego is *nimugu* (male or female) to a woman (*nimugu*) who is minmin of ego's tamak, and hence, like tamak, is in a position to exchange rather than share nurture as a paternal substance relationship. Unlike tamak, however, ego's nimugu (as tamak's minmin) interacts with ego in a joking, playful, "plundering" relationship. Ego is *egohup* (male or female) to a person of the opposite sex who is ego's tamak's tata, and this is also a cross-unit, exchanging relationship. Egohups must show restraint and general avoidance toward one another. Ego is *pavugu* (male or female) to another person of the same sex who is also tata to ego's tamak. Like nimugus, pavugus "plunder" and joke with one another.

Ego is *tumbugu* (male or female) to another male or female (*tumbugu*) through a variety of categorical interrelationships. Tumbugus may share within the same social unit, as for example, ego and his or her nanga's nanga. Tumbugus, as *"ewenteburubuns,"* exchange with one another in cross-unit relationships. Ewenteburubun tumbugus also joke with one another in a reflection of the nimugu and pavugu categories.

In the remainder of this chapter, social categories are considered in terms of Mandak normative expectations of interactions in these relationships. Preceding each discussion is a quoted definition of the category as recorded from a Mandak man's answer to my question: "what *is* nanga (example?)." The categories which express maternal nurture are considered first: nanga/emandak, nanga/enek, minmin/minmin, tata/tata, metak/metak. These are followed by explications of categories communicating paternal substance: tamak/emandak, tamak/enek, nimugu/nimugu, pavugu/pavugu, egohup/egohup. The tumbugu category includes symbolic forms of either maternal nurture or paternal substance. Affinal nurture social categories will be considered in chapter 4.

SHARING NURTURE

Nanga/Emandak, Nanga/Enek

> *"Evene numi ivasik momoton nyia ma niya iriri agugi nanga."*
>
> "This woman procreates true me and I call, I call her nanga."

Entailed attributes of the nanga/emandak, nanga/enek categories are: (*a*) nanga is female, the reciprocal is either male (emandak) or female (enek); (*b*) the dyad is a same-moiety, nonmarriageable relationship. By entailed attributes I mean the minimal criteria necessary for persons to assume a particular relationship.

Nanga marks the beginning of a series of female relationships which share maternal nurture with ego. For male ego the series proceeds from procreating female to procreating female: nanga-minmin-female-tata; while for female ego it is nanga-metak-enek-tumbugu (figure 2). At the end of both series, one "begins again:" when male ego's female tata marries, she becomes "nanga" to him, and the child of female ego's female tumbugu is *enek aulit*. Aulit means "to start again," "to come back." The Mandak recognize this series of women who through procreation provide new members for the ebibinet, although it is not a unit or group which is named or has any particular social function.

The nanga category expresses the maternal nurture symbol. According to Mandak definitions, nanga is the female who procreates ego. It is a nurturing relationship, with food, care, protection, and wealth given by nanga to emandak and enek. When asked to distinguish a foster nanga from the woman who actually gave birth to ego, the Mandak refer to the former as "the nanga who made me grow, made me large." The nurturing aspect of the nanga relationship is enacted soon after birth when the "true" nanga or a classificatory nanga gives masticated taro to the newborn child to ensure a healthy beginning. She is the first to introduce this primary "cultural food" to the infant in an act which reiterates the symbolic associations between female, taro, and ebibinet, interrelated idioms of maternal nurture.

Emandak and enek are members of the ebibinet of *nanga momoton* ("true"), the woman who actually gave birth to them.

Offspring do not share physiological substance with nanga, but instead take from her their first important and necessary sustenance during gestation. In analyzing the Mandak procreation ideology, I was frustrated at first by the blank looks that always followed my question: "What does a person receive from his nanga [in procreation]?" While people had ready answers about what was received from the procreating father, many could not find an appropriate response at all to the nanga question, although a few ventured "the ebibinet name" as that which is received from nanga. I concluded that the question did not make sense to the Mandak, for, as will become clear in later discussions of the tamak category, nothing is "received" from nanga. "Receiving" entails giving, prestations, indebtedness, and exchanges: a person "partakes" of nurture from nanga. To give and receive implies separate entities, while partaking, sharing, and being of one kind are the appropriate terms to use in describing the nanga/emandak and nanga/enek relationships.

The normative role of nanga is to provide a continuous source of nurture to emandak and enek. This begins in the womb and continues after birth through nursing, provision of taro and other foods, and general care and protection. Although the idiom ebolout ("womb") is not used to identify or refer to nanga, the erus ("breast, breast milk") idiom is appropriate to this relationship. In speaking of a nanga bond, a person does not say "I came from her womb," but instead says "She nursed me, gave me milk." Provision of nurture through nursing is a focal expression of the nanga category. Several women told me that they had nursed their adopted offspring. Although no examples occurred while I was in Pinikindu, people claimed that a woman who has not given birth can produce milk by applying heat and certain medicinal plants to her breasts. The Mandak often refer to nursing as a definitive feature of the nanga role. For example, in 1970 two women were fighting over the custody of a five-year-old boy. One of the women, the child's father's sister, had cared for the boy since he was about eight months old. When the child's "true" nanga requested her son's return, the foster nanga refused, stating that she was the appropriate nanga since she had fed and cared for the boy for some years and had even nursed him back to health by making milk come to her own breasts. The foster nanga succeeded in keeping the boy.

While a person who performs the normative aspects of the nanga role may be called "nanga," a child cannot be recruited to a woman's clan by "fostering." Two examples will illustrate this point. First, there is the case just mentioned in which the foster nanga was the child's father's sister. The latter's ebibinet was headed by an influential Big Man but was a small, declining clan with no procreating women. The adopted boy, however, continues to be a member of the social unit of the woman who gave birth to him. Although the latter, a Papuan woman, does not yet belong to any ebibinet, her emandak is a member of her undetermined social unit. When he is an adult, he may join another clan (not his foster nanga's, since it is in the opposite moiety) by exchanging for it, as will be explained in chapter 5.

A second foster nanga situation illustrates the separation of primary and secondary nurturing in relation to the nanga role and ebibinet recruitment. A woman, A, of Kontabut ebibinet was fostered by a woman of Lentila ebibinet, both of Erangam moiety. A grew up, married, and produced ten children, some of whom now also have offspring. A and her children have tried to establish claims to Lentila membership because the ebibinet owns much land in Pinikindu, while Kontabut has no land in the immediate area. A told me that she was "half" Lentila since the woman who had nursed her as an infant was a member of Lentila. People have steadfastly refuted her claims to even "partial" Lentila membership. When one of her adult sons planted coconut trees on Lentila land, the old woman who had nursed his mother pulled up all his newly planted coconut shoots. Although the community agrees that A and her children have the right to use Lentila land temporarily for gardens or residence, they have no permanent claim, as is implied by planting coconut trees, for they do not belong to Lentila clan. Although the nanga category is assumed by women who perform the role's nurturing function, a woman cannot recruit her foster emandak-enek to her ebibinet. This does not mean that social organization in Mandak society is not flexible enough to meet the exigencies of human life, for there are ways in which people may be adopted into an ebibinet. But it cannot be done through the nanga category.

In normative terms the nanga category expresses maternal nurture, but its moral force varies in strength according to whether the dyad is a moiety, ebibinet, or ewentus relationship. The moral force of maternal nurture is greatest between nanga and emandak-enek of the same ewentus, and least at the moiety level. Nanga and emandak-enek of the same ewentus are expected to share nurture to a greater extent than nanga and emandak-enek belonging only to the same moiety. Within the same ewentus, the dyad forms a unit which acts together in exchanges with others in cross-unit relationships. The nature and contexts of these exchanges are discussed in chapter 5.

In summary, the normative role of the nanga category is one in which food, care, protection, and sustenance are provided by the nanga (female) for emandak (male) and enek (female). The direction of nurturing is from nanga to emandak-enek, and it is regarded as a continuous process within a dyad which is of *one kind* and which expresses maternal nurture.

Minmin/Minmin

"Neni num evene enges evene gabasik nima, niya anagugi minmin."

"She this woman, one woman procreated us, I call her minmin."

The entailed attributes of the minmin category are: (*a*) it is a cross-sex relationship, and (*b*) minmins belong to the same moiety and cannot marry one another. An alternative term, which is said to be more traditional among the Mandak, is *inegu*. Today, however, inegu is used in address less often than the minmin form.

The minmin category is a culturally important relationship which epitomizes major elements of the Mandak social symbolizations. The category expresses maternal nurture: persons in a minmin relationship are defined as male and female who share one womb. While siblings may also share one father, paternal substance is not used to define the minmin bond. For example, when referring to a minmin relationship between two persons who share the same father but have different mothers, one would not say, "they share one blood," but instead would use a maternal nurture expression such as, "they are of one womb," or "they are of one breast."

The maternal nurture metaphor communicates relationships devoted to a continuous sharing of food, wealth, and so forth (nurture). Sexual intercourse and marriage are excluded from these relationships. Although members within maternal nurture units sustain and support one another, they cannot initiate membership growth through procreation, since such recruitment depends on cross-unit paternal substance relationships. The minmin category involves a male-female dyad, both members of which obtain maternal nurture from the same source, nanga, and between whom sex and marriage are forbidden. Physical and social interaction between minmins is circumscribed, with an emphasis on the cross-sex nature of the bond. The relationship is governed by strongly sanctioned norms enjoining avoidance and respect, while at the same time it is a category emphasizing sharing and "being of one kind." I will concentrate here on the latter features and reserve discussion of the cross-sex taboos for chapter 4.

A woman should be constantly concerned with her minmin's welfare. As the major way in which the Mandak show concern, she should make frequent gifts of food to his household. Since the relationship entails physical avoidance, minmins never actually eat together, nor does a woman hand food directly to her minmin. Typically, a woman will take cooked taro or sweet potatoes to her minmin's house and give it to his wife with the message that the food is for her minmin's child. Through such actions, the Mandak say, it is understood that the woman is actually thinking of her minmin, but the state of avoidance between them necessitates expressions of indirect sharing.

Food always moves from female to male minmin. The male's normative role is to make exchanges on behalf of his female minmin with her husband's ebibinet. The male-exchanging, female-sharing dichotomy expressed by the minmin dyad is formalized in the custom of *erembeke*. Although moiety status can never be altered among the Mandak, through erembeke a woman may change her ebibinet membership within the same moiety. To effect such a change through erembeke, a woman must belong to an ebibinet with no male members, or more typically, be an immigrant into a village where she has no clan members. Erembeke allows a woman to "adopt" a man of her own moiety as her minmin. If she is from "far away," the new minmin relationship also means that the woman and her offspring become members of the minmin's ebibinet. If a woman already has clan members in the village or in neighboring villages, she may initiate a new minmin relationship by erembeke simply to emphasize the moral force of maternal nurture with a man of her own moiety but different ebibinet.

In the custom of erembeke, a woman takes food regularly to her chosen minmin's household. No formal or public announcement is made of erembeke or of the new minmin relationship. This relationship cannot be effected quickly, but involves two to three years of interaction whereby food is given by a woman to her sought-after minmin's household. This is appropriate to the concept of nurture, whereby social support, growth, and continuity must be founded on foundations of demonstrated relationships. After food has been shared for some time, the adoptive relationship is validated by the gradual assumption of proper category terms and behavior between the man and woman and other interrelated persons. An important feature of this validation occurs when the man makes exchanges on behalf of his new minmin, generally at a death feast in which the woman has affinal obligations to provide food or wealth.

The following case illustrates erembeke. A Pinikindu man, Timot of Tuwaram ebibinet (Emalam), married a Tolai woman from Rabaul. This woman henceforth was classified as Erangam, but she lacked local ebibinet affiliations. After the couple had lived in Pinikindu for several years, the Tolai woman began taking cooked taro or sweet potatoes several times a week to the household of Selatien, a man of Meamea ebibinet, Erangam moiety. Timot noticed these food gifts, and people said he was happy that his wife was choosing a minmin who would later contribute food and pigs to Tuwaram death feasts. For several years the Tolai woman continued to give food to Selatien's household. After a time, Selatien began to extend minmin respect to her, addressing her as "minmin" rather than by her personal name. His wife and other persons also called her by the appropriate category terms. Several years after erembeke had begun, a Tuwaram man died and Selatien contributed a pig worth seventy dollars to one of the death feasts. This exchange signified to the community that the Tolai woman and Selatien were truly minmins, that, as one man said, "they are of one womb now."

It is important, the Mandak say, for a woman to have a minmin, for if she doesn't, who would make the appropriate exchanges for her when her ebibinet has obligations to another social unit? It is important to note here that the way a woman effects a new maternal nurture relationship is through giving food to a male, thereby acting out an important aspect of this metaphor. She thus participates in the continuous nurturance of the ebibinet, a focal symbolic expression of "being of one kind."

Tata/Tata

> *"Ilya kanlago ine ne nanga."*
>
> "He is minmin of nanga."

The entailed attributes of the tata category are: (*a*) it is a male/male or male/female dyad, (*b*) the individuals belong to the same moiety and are in a nonmarriageable relationship. Alternative terms for the category are *noiyak* and *evelom*.

The minmin of nanga, as several persons defined tata, expresses elements of maternal nurture. In accordance with the food-giving idiom of this female nurture symbol, sustenance flows to the tata dyad from a woman who is minmin to one and nanga to the other. They are linked to the same nurturing source as "person" and also to the same maternal nurture unit, whether at the ewentus, ebibinet, or moiety level. Persons in a tata relationship share food, wealth, and so on (nurture), while the moral force of sharing decreases in strength according to the dyad's membership in an ewentus, ebibinet, or moiety.

Two factors impinge on the tata category in regard to its expression of maternal nurture. First, in normative terms the nurturing member of the dyad is male, the minmin of nanga, so that there is no enactment of food-giving from female to male as in minmin and nanga relationships. As one man stated in explaining the normative role of tata, "The tata 'looks nothing' on his minmin's children." By this he meant that the tata does not make formal, public gifts of food or wealth to his minmin's children. Although wealth and property are shared between tatas, no rituals emphasize their maternal nurture bonds.

The second factor that influences symbolic expressions in the tata category is the frequent coexistence of important authority relationships within the dyad. As minmin of nanga, tata is often elder male to his minmin's offspring. In the general constellation of power in Mandak society, male precedes female, older dominates younger. As minmin of nanga, tata commonly stands in a relationship of diffuse power over his minmin's children. This inequality was reflected in former times by differential terms of address: minmin's children called their nanga's minmin "tata," while the reciprocal address form was "noiyak" or "evelom." Today, however, the latter usages are heard infrequently and the reciprocal "tata" is the common form. The diffuse power inequality becomes more specific when both tatas belong to the same ewentus or ebibinet and when the elder is also the major decision-maker of his social unit. However, the kind of authority that older tata exerts over younger should not be confused with the socializing discipline by which tamak nurtures his offspring. The authority of elder tata toward his minmin's children is restricted to social unit affairs, matters involving land use and exchanges at marriages, deaths, and other feasts—contexts in which the person acts as a member of a social unit rather than as an individual. An elder tata should also teach his minmin's offspring about ebibinet matters. He is expected to pass on important knowledge and skills such as fishing or sorcery to his younger tatas in order to preserve this wealth within the ebibinet. Such "inheritance" expresses elements of the maternal nurture symbol, the sharing expected between persons in a bounded unit who work for one another's continued well-being through mutual protection and sustenance.

A female tata, enek of minmin, becomes "nanga" to her tata when she marries, while he assumes the emandak reciprocal. This is done, people explain, so that the series may "begin again," the nanga-minmin-tata series of females belonging to male ego's maternal nurture unit. The relationship of differential authority remains the same, however, with older male over younger female, although, as in the normative nanga/emandak category, female tata when married assumes a food-giving relationship to emandak.

Metak/Metak

> *"Enges evene gabasik nima anagugi metak."*
>
> "One woman procreated us, I call him metak."

Metak is one of the broadest of Mandak social categories in that it encompasses a wider range of entailed criteria than most of the others. It may include dyads of male/male, female/female, or through marriage, male/female, and such persons may be of the same or opposite moiety and stand in marriageable or nonmarriageable relationship to one another. However, as a form expressing symbolic elements, the metak category may be defined as a single-sex dyad governed by maternal nurture, with an emphasis on sharing, cooperation, and being of one kind.

Metaks are defined generally by the Mandak as persons of the same sex who are procreated by the same nanga. As with minmin, paternal substance idioms are not used to express the metak relationship. Metaks receive maternal nurture from the same source, nanga, and represent only one side of the sexual dichotomy, whether female/female or male/male. I will discuss first the normative features of the metak category as a single-sex, same moiety dyad and then consider other relationships incorporated within the category.

In normative terms, cooperation, sharing, and informality are definitive features of the metak category. No cross-sex restrictions inhibit interaction between persons in this relationship. Metak share more attributes than people in other social categories, being of one sex, partaking of the same source of maternal nurture, and standing in the same position to paternal substance and affinal nurture relationships. As in other categories, however, the moral force of the metak relationship is strongest within the ewentus and becomes progressively weaker at the moiety level. Within the same ewentus and ebibinet, metaks form a group "of one kind," for being of the same sex they occupy similar positions in the division of labor, activities, rituals, and space accorded to the different sexes (chap. 4). Partaking of the same maternal nurture source, "belonging to the same womb or breast," they also share multiple responsibilities and obligations of social unit membership. Metaks are expected to cooperate in work projects: females in gardening, males in heavy garden work and fishing. They thus often use one another's property: baskets, shell knives, and digging sticks among the women, fishing gear among the men. Metaks should also help one another with exchanges, whether they are the shared responsibility of the same social unit or are in relation to affinal clans or subclans. In the first case, for example, at tamak's death feast only one or two of a metak group will make the necessary pig contributions and payments for paternal substance, although the prestations erase the debt for all the metaks. While these payments are made in the name of only one or two persons, all the metaks act together to compile the exchange. They also form a unit to revenge injury to one of their number or social group, whether from physical or verbal fights or from sorcery. For example, in a feud I observed between a man and his son-in-law, many of the threats between the pair centered on the relative strength of their metaks.

Metak relationships within the same ewentus or ebibinet often entail a degree of informally recognized age and power differences. Since metaks frequently act as a unit in work, exchanges, or revenge, there must be some means to arrive at joint decisions. Usually the eldest takes responsibility for initiating common actions and making decisions. Such direction of group activity may be only in relation to situations that are a direct part of social unit obligations, or it may also encompass daily work activities. This variability seems to depend on the political aspirations and power of the eldest metak. For example, one group of male metaks who shared the same father and mother cooperated irregularly in daily work routines and worked together consistently only in regard to ewentus exchange obligations. The oldest metak was not regarded as a rising Big Man and displayed little political ambition. Another male metak group, belonging to one ebibinet but different subclans, cooperated frequently in both subsistence and exchange endeavors. In this case the eldest was an ambitious and powerful Big Man in the community.

The definitive features of the metak category involve an emphasis on maternal nurture sharing and cooperation: on "being of one kind" in relation to other distinctions of nurture and sex. Metaks share the same position both in the sexual dichotomy and in the nurturing structure of social relations.

Through relationships of marriage and formalized "friendship," the metak category also includes persons who do not share the same source of maternal nurture. The metak category is extended reciprocally at marriage by male ego to his wife's metaks and by female ego to her husband's metaks. There is thus in marriage a categorical merging by ego of his metaks and their spouses and his spouse's metaks with his own metaks. While these relationships involve cross-sex, cross-moiety dyads, the normative focus remains the same, with an emphasis on cooperation, informality, and sharing. Symbolically they are "single sex" relationships without the "shame" emphasized in certain other cross-sex, cross-moiety relationships (chapter 4). Members of affinally created metak dyads respond to one another, in the normative sense, as if they were of the same sex. For example, one man when asked why he called his metak's wife "metak" said it was because he could go at any time to his male metak's house and if the latter weren't there, he could ask the man's spouse for food and eat it with her as if she were his male metak. For male and female to eat together generally has connotations of sexual intimacy like that between husband and wife. Extensions of the metak category to the reciprocal's spouse thus allows informal interaction and cooperation between households of metaks, in contrast to relations between households of minmins. This usage also accords with the precontact preference for the levirate and sororate in second marriages after a spouse's death.

A category which partakes of the same normative features as metak is *naak*. Two men or women who marry metaks of the same ebibinet become "naak" to one another. They may also refer to each other as "metak" as an alternative. The normative emphasis in the naak relationship is on sharing, cooperation, and informality. Persons in this category share maternal nurture before their marriages, being of the same moiety, and marriage into the same ebibinet strengthens the moral force of their previous sharing bond. Naaks occupy similar structural positions in relation to the same affinal nurture social unit. They share cross-unit responsibilities, both contributing paternal substance or exchanging affinal nurture with the same ebibinet, or both. In normative terms, naaks should help one another in such activities as exchanges and feasts. A person may also call the spouse of his or her *nimugu* "naak," or "metak," another instance of two persons brought into a strengthened maternal nurture relationship through cross-unit obligations to the same clan. Before the colonial restrictions on polygamous unions, a man would call a co-husband "metak" and a woman would call her co-wife "metak."

Another category which has been likened to metak is *ewentamat.* Ewentamats are male members of the same moiety who have formalized a relationship of mutual cooperation. They often belong to different villages, and the bond serves as a way to extend cooperative networks for aid in feasts and exchanges. An ewentamat relationship is initiated by reciprocal feasts and exchanges between the dyad. A man invites a prospective ewentamat to his hamlet for a small feast at which he gives the latter a shell valuable and makes a speech about the desired ewentamat bond. If such a relationship is accepted by the guest, he will later reciprocate with a feast, public speech, and shell money of equal value. Henceforth the two men will cooperate in the same spirit as metaks of the same ebibinet. The relationship cannot be broken except by the death of one of the partners.

Marriage and Maternal Nurture

In addition to the categories that have been discussed, there are others—*nenak, namuna, nalun* (see table 1)—which also express elements of maternal nurture. *Nenak* involves dyads of a woman and her spouse's tamak or nanga and thus expresses maternal nurture in the same-moiety relationship and affinal nurture in the opposite-moiety dyad. Again the normative emphasis is on mutual helpfulness, informality, and cooperation. The moral force of this relationship is relatively weak in that little emphasis is placed on its normative features, in contrast, for example, to the naak category. In short, people had little to say about nenak behavior and interaction.

The *namuna* category includes a man and his spouse's tamak or his enek's spouse. Both belong to the same maternal nurture unit (moiety) and thus are in a sharing relationship. They have married into the same social unit or have married a dyad of nanga/enek, a closely cooperative female maternal nurture bond. Here, too, the normative emphasis is on sharing and mutual aid. However, namunas are less "of one kind" than naaks, since they stand in different relationships to each other's spouse and hence may be at cross-purposes in various social interests and obligations.

The *nalun* category reflects the naak relationship in that the former involves women who have married men who are tatas to one another. The members of the nalun dyad are related through maternal nurture before marriage, a bond which then strengthens the moral force of their sharing. They are often cross-unit nurturing adjuncts to the same ebibinet and as such are expected to work together in their spouses' feasts and ceremonies. Each nalun stands in an avoidance relationship to the other's husband.

SUMMARY

The major social categories expressing maternal nurture are nanga, tata, minmin, and metak. In terms of nurturing relationships, ego receives primary female nurture from nanga. Nanga/emandak and nanga/enek communicate at the person-to-person level the central meaning of the maternal nurture metaphor. From the nanga relationship are derived the sharing categories of minmin and metak, both defined as partaking with ego of the same source of maternal nurture. The sexual dichotomy is emphasized in the contrast between minmin and metak. Minmin is a cross-sex dyad entailing "shame," with a complementary balance of male-exchanging and female-sharing. Metak, being a single-sex dyad, is an undifferentiated category, a maternal nurture group "of one kind" treated as a unit. In the relationship of a man to his minmin's offspring, tata represents an extension of sharing through minmin. With marriage, a variety of relationships are initiated—metak, naak, nalun, nenak, and namuna—in which the moral force of maternal nurture sharing is strengthened.

EXCHANGING NURTURE

Tamak/Emandak, Tamak/Enek

> *"Erandi gavukay ne nanga ma neni num erandi*
> *gabasigia ma niya agugi tamak."*

> "A man married nanga and he, this man,
> procreated me and I call him tamak."

The entailed attributes of the tamak/emandak and tamak/enek categories include: (*a*) it is a male/male or male/female dyad, and (*b*) persons in the relationship belong to opposite moieties.

The tamak category expresses paternal substance. Tamak is the male agent who joins with nanga to procreate emandak and enek. Not only does tamak provide the initial substance of his emandak and enek, but after their births, tamak also helps "grow" (nurture) them. Thus, in the tamak relationship food, shelter, wealth, protection, magic, and skills are rightfully given by tamak to his emandak and enek as prestations of nurture.

Tamak rather than tata plays the major male role in socializing Mandak children. Imparting social mores, fishing skills, and other kinds of knowledge is part of tamak's nurturing role. Today such socialization obligations also include paying school fees for emandak and enek, a not inconsiderable portion of a man's yearly income.

Tamak's nurturing role may be illustrated by several cases in which the category has been assumed by individuals who lack the usual criteria for the position—who are not enmeshed in the local framework of social relationships. After we had been living in Pinikindu for several months, one of the men in the village began addressing me as enek. At first I was puzzled by this adoption, since the man was only ten years my senior. One day as several men were eating a fish catch on the beach, my adoptive tamak handed me a portion of the cooked food. As he did so, he explained to one of his companions that he was feeding me because I was his "enek," whom he was "procreating" (gabasik). Then it became clear that he had been relating to me as tamak by bringing food to our house frequently and in this way nurturing me.

While we were in Pinikindu, another adoption illustrated the importance of nurturing in the tamak role. My husband and I were frequent guests at the hamlet of a middle-aged man who was teaching us many aspects of Mandak customs. To reciprocate for his help and hospitality, we bought several things for him when we went to Kavieng for supplies. The day after we had presented these gifts, he referred to us as "mommy" and "poppy," his English translations of nanga and tamak. We were both somewhat confused by suddenly being placed in a parental category by a man many years older than ourselves until we realized that it was based on our recent behavior of giving him things and thus nurturing him.

Other behavioral enactments of the tamak relationship occur again and again between Mandak men and New Guinea workers from nearby plantations. In Neo-Melanesian terms, a friendship between a local man and one of these workers is a *papa-pikinini* relationship. In such cases a local man befriends a plantation worker, who then spends much of his free time at the local man's hamlet as a guest for meals and receives small gifts such as betel and tobacco. Here, again, "papa," the Neo-Melanesian translation of tamak, is the one who feeds and provides for his pikinini (emandak).

Nurture bonds between tamak and his emandak and enek include not only regular gifts of sustenance but also may involve the transfer of land rights. While land is the property of the ebibinet and ewentus, it is also an aspect of bilateral nurture, a source of sustenance. Traditionally a man could give part of his ebibinet land to his offspring, although the major portions of land remained with the owning ebibinet. This practice has been complicated, though not abandoned, by the Australian government, which read a strictly matrilineal interpretation into local customs and decreed that a man must pay for all land transfers out of the clan. This law frustrates and angers the Mandak, since although ebibinet members have primary rights to their social unit lands, such property may be derived secondarily through the tamak relationship, in accordance with the concept that nurture is given by both tamak and nanga.

The tamak category serves as the principal vehicle of paternal substance relationships between social units and other categories. Tamak crosses maternal nurture boundaries to provide the substance of emandak and enek—to initiate their procreation. More important, in Mandak cultural priorities, is the nurturing role of tamak and his ewentus in the growth and development of emandak and enek. This cross-unit nurture establishes a debt for tamak's offspring and their social unit to their paternal substance ewentus. While tamak's relationship to his emandak and enek has the appearance of sharing, it differs from nanga's nurture in the sense of indebtedness which surrounds it. For example, I often listened to men complain of the work involved in providing for offspring; yet I never heard a nanga lament the food, work, and wealth given to her children. Nurture can be shared only by those related through maternal nurture. When nurture is extended through paternal substance or marriage bonds, it must ultimately be repaid.

Tamak is the male link between ebibinets, the creator of blood ties between social units. While blood is a symbolic idiom expressing relationship between units connected by procreation, exchange between these units is expressed as payment for nurture, for the care and provision given by tamak and his social unit to his emandak and enek and their social unit. While a person pays off blood for cross-unit nurture, such exchanges do not erase these consanguineal bonds, which may be called forth for a variety of cooperative ventures. The major exchange for paternal substance occurs at tamak's death feast (chap. 5). Therefore, tamak as an individual does not actually receive compensation for his own cross-unit nurturing; rather, his social unit is the receptor of payments for their extension of "sharing" in the paternal substance relationship. One man stated the normative aspects of the category as follows:

> When tamak is living, everything is hard work, he must work hard to get fish, coconuts, sweet potatoes, taro, and other things. He doesn't think about his own ebibinet, but his thoughts are only for his children. Now when tamak dies, his children must return, pay back for this care and provision.

In terms of prestations of food and minor gifts, a man should think first of his emandak and enek and only second of his minmin's offspring, the children of his own ebibinet. For example, on Christmas Day we stayed at the household of a man who had four sons and one male tata, all under age ten and living in the same hamlet. The man made a formal presentation of candy to the children. He lined them up, his sons first, his tata last, and explained that in all such matters it had to be this way—his tata must "come last." This matter of precedence was governed not by sentiment but by the norm that for tamak, paternal substance nurture should in certain respects come before maternal nurture sharing. This applies only to the giving of food and minor wealth, since land, major wealth, pigs, shell valuables, and important magical skills should remain in the ebibinet. However, if no ebibinet members are available to inherit major wealth it may be passed on to a man's blood relations, especially to his emandak and enek. For example, an elderly man was discussing who would take over his hamlet after his death, since he lacked local ebibinet members. His only minmin had married and moved down the coast to another village. He thought, however, that this minmin and her children would accept the idea of his own children taking over his hamlet when he died because his minmin knew that these children "had not come up as weeds of the bush," but that he "had made them come up"—through paternal substance nurturing. When they own his hamlet grounds, these children will still not be members of their tamak's ebibinet.

Tamak is an affine to ego in the sense that it is a relationship involving marriage into ego's maternal nurture unit. Some individuals defined tamak as "the man who married my nanga and procreated me." Nanga would never be defined as "the woman who married my tamak" because definitions using "to marry" imply a cross-unit relationship, one in which nurture crosses maternal nurture boundaries and necessitates an exchange. As will be discussed in chapter 5, when tamak dies the payments expected from both tamak's spouse and his offspring may be represented by a single exchange, thus recognizing both affinal nurture and paternal substance relationships between the two social units.

Nimugu/Nimugu

"Num evene waynedu mine tamak ma niya anaromi nimugu."

"This woman, two minmins with tamak, and I call her nimugu."

The entailed attributes of the nimugu category are: (*a*) the dyad is female/female or female/male, (*b*) it is a cross-unit relationship between members of opposite moieties.

The nimugu category complements tamak/emandak and tamak/enek in terms of relative emphasis on paternal substance nurturing and paternal substance exchanging. While the normative aspects of tamak focus on the giving of nurture, nimugu expresses the cross-unit indebtedness involved in paternal substance bonds. Offspring of nimugu's minmin are reminded in various public rituals of their debt to their blood relations for nurture. Such reminders are carried out in interactions of joking and "play," with the initiative for joking a prerogative of the minmin of ego's tamak. One man described nimugu as "my nimugu is the same as my wife—there can be no shame between us." Nimugu behaves informally with her minmin's children: she touches, teases, and plays with them, sits on their laps, and pulls at their laplaps. Male and female nimugus may sleep in the same room and eat together. Such intimacies do not include sexual intercourse, although a kind of sexual teasing is part of the normative relationship between nimugus of the opposite sex and of the same sex in certain ritual contexts. For example, during one celebration when people were dancing to a string band, each person separately, I observed two nimugus, male and female, dancing together in close embrace. Such public intimacy between members of the opposite sex would be scandalous in other cross-sex categories, even between spouses.

Nimugu joking behavior communicates a state of indebtedness between units related by paternal substance. It is nimugu's role to ritually remind her minmin's offspring that they are consuming nurture from her social unit through their tamak relationship. The Mandak describe nimugu's intentions in her "play" with her minmin's children as being joyful and proud of her paternal substance connections. People interpreted most nimugu acts, such as throwing ashes on her minmin's children, as the result not of anger but of nimugu's happiness at the sight of her ebibinet's substance.

Many public eating occasions provide a setting for nimugu rituals. A woman may suddenly stand up during such gatherings, perform a shuffling dance, and with raucous song present a small gift of food to one of her minmin's children. In the cases I witnessed, the recipient always looked shamefaced and accepted the gift without speaking, amid the laughter of the surrounding group. Such gestures of food-giving suggest a kind of mock public nurturing act which expresses cross-unit paternal substance relationships. While both tamak's regular food gifts to his children and nimugu's minor gifts are aspects of paternal substance, the former form a part of continuous sustenance, the latter a kind of cackling reminder of the food that is being passed across ebibinet lines.

On the occasion of an *egirimis* feast, which will be discussed in chapter 5, nimugu presents food to her minmin's child. When an egirimis is held to mark the birth of a couple's first child, tamak's minmin gives two taro plants to the parents of her new nimugu. The taro is planted by the mother of the child, and when he is an adult he will be given cuttings to plant in his own garden. The Mandak explanation is again that nimugu is rejoicing over the appearance of blood. The prestation is another expression of cross-unit nurturing by paternal substance relationships. In this case taro, with its associations of female, ebibinet, and maternal nurture, is passed across social unit boundaries to follow an extension of nurture.

When a person belonging to her ebibinet dies, nimugu puts ashes on the faces and shoulders of her minmin's children. This act is performed with mock humor and the recipients look shamefaced. The latter give their nimugu a small payment of one shilling, which is said to "stop" the action, this recognition of blood by nimugu. One man elaborated on this act by saying that nimugu is reminding her minmin's children that they are consuming food from her ebibinet, but that they shouldn't worry, for she is not angry. Here again, it is nimugu's role to publicly state the food-taking relationship of blood ties, the transfer of nurture across unit boundaries. The small payment made to nimugu when she marks them with ashes may be regarded as a token exchange by the indebted minmin's children to their tamak's ebibinet. This exchange recognizes the cross-unit rather than same-unit nature of the paternal substance relationship. The custom of placing ashes and receiving shilling payments at the time of a death is extended so that ultimately everyone of the deceased's moiety may put ashes on anyone of the opposite moiety.

The nimugu category thus functions as an expression of the indebtedness of an ewentus and ebibinet to the social unit which gave it substance and nurture. Nimugu communicates her symbolic statement, however, in a joking manner through public gifts of food to her minmin's children or by playful interaction with them. In addition to the general teasing informality between nimugus, a woman has plunder rights to anything belonging to her minmin's children—laplaps, lime baskets, flashlights—and neither anger nor regret should be shown by the owners of the lost property.

At nimugu's death, her minmin's children wash, clean, dress, and bury the body. If there are no minmin's children, persons in another blood relationship to the deceased perform these duties. This act establishes an interesting symmetry in cross-unit relationships: tamak initiates a person's procreation, and that person performs the final actions in regard to substance at the death of tamak's minmin. Between social units, therefore, the gift of substance is complemented by the burial of substance.

As in other social categories, there are varying degrees of moral force in the normative aspects of the nimugu category. The strongest moral force is found at the level of subclans connected by marriage and procreation, the weakest at the moiety level between persons not directly connected by interunit marriages.

Pavugu/Pavugu

> *"Num erandi welabanan du mine tamak, ma*
> *niya agugi wepavugu nima, num erandi."*
>
> "This man, two tatas with tamak, and
> I call us two pavugus, this man."

The entailed attributes of the pavugu category are: (*a*) it is a single-sex dyad, male/male, female/female, and (*b*) the individuals belong to different moieties.

The Mandak definition of pavugu as "my tamak is his or her

tata" identifies pavugu with ego's tamak. Pavugu shares maternal nurture with ego's tamak and stands in a relationship of paternal substance to ego. Persons in the pavugu category are related through bilateral nurture, since they both partake of nurture from the same individual who is tata to one, tamak to the other. Although in a logical sense, following the procreation ideology, pavugus do not share substance, according to Mandak symbolic distinctions, pavugu is a blood relationship.

As in the nimugu category, normative interactions between pavugus involve play and joking. The right to initiate joking is the prerogative of ego's tamak's tata, although ego may reciprocate with similar behavior. Much of the play between pavugus revolves around minor plunders, taking of small objects such as knives, flashlights, and tin containers. I discovered that it was almost impossible to give individuals any lasting presents, for within a day or two a gift was usually possessed by the recipient's pavugu.

It is imperative in the pavugu relationship that plunder rights be taken in good humor, and in most cases people appeared to enjoy pavugu jokes. However, at times plunder assumes major propor- tions, and it becomes an effort for those involved to maintain the normative jollity. People like to recount a particular incident of pavugu behavior which took place several years ago. A man, A, bought a bicycle, an expensive and cherished item not owned by many Mandak. A few days after the purchase, however, his pavugu took the bicycle in a demonstration of "plunder" rights. Although his wife raged, outwardly A maintained good humor over the incident. After several months, his pavugu began preparing for his tri-annual sale of copra. On the night when the copra was finally ready for market, A brought a celebration bottle of whisky to his pavugu, who soon became drunk and fell into a deep sleep. Meanwhile, A loaded the sacks of dried coconut into a hired truck, drove to Kavieng, and sold the copra for eighty dollars. The bicycle had cost only about forty dollars. Again, good pavugu composure was displayed by the "victim," although his wife and other hamlet relatives were quite angry.

There are other forms of pavugu play. At any feast, for example, a man or woman may tamper with his/her pavugu's food by adding too much salt or hot peppers or in other ways making it unpalatable. During dances at a final death feast, a man or woman may slap white powdered lime on the back of a pavugu, who later reciprocates with a stick of tobacco or one shilling. When a man marries for the first time, his tamak's male tata has plunder rights to anything in the groom's house. This joking action cannot be performed in reverse.

The Mandak explanation for pavugu joking is that ego's pavugu is his blood relation and that it was pavugu's tata who "made ego come up." The normative pavugu relationship involves ego's indebtedness to his/her tamak's tata for nurture consumed from tamak's ebibinet. This is expressed in both pavugu and nimugu categories by mock plunder and a normative emphasis on joking and play. It is also seen in ego's obligation to respond to his/her pavugu's (tamak's tata) demands for assistance in exchanges, feast preparations, or other activities. While ego may also aid his/her tata's offspring in such undertakings, the emphasis is on ego's responsibilities toward his/her tamak's tata.

While pavugu emphasizes indebtedness in paternal substance relationships, the category also expresses the nurturing elements of the symbol. Pavugu is said to be "the same as metak" in the normative focus on informality and cooperation within the dyad. I suggest that this aspect of the pavugu relationship derives from their partaking of the same nurture. Pavugus receive sustenance from the same source, who is tamak to one, tata to the other. In the normative relationship, they cooperate in a kind of pale reflection of the metak category. Because they derive from different kinds of nurture, however, the relationship departs from the sharing of metaks to the joking, plunder, and play between pavugus.

Egohup/Egohup

> *"Num evene wetata ndu mine num erandi tamak,*
> *num erandi mi tamakarak gabasigia ma*
> *neni noina num niya ariri mi egohuparak evene"*

"This woman, two tatas with this man tamak, this man my tamak
    procreated me and she his tata I call my egohup, woman."

The entailed attributes of the egohup category are: (*a*) the dyad is a cross-sex relationship, and (*b*) the individuals belong to opposite moieties.

The egohup category is similar to the pavugu relationship in that the dyad derives nurture from the same source, who is tamak to one and tata to the other. However, the egohup category involves a cross-sex relationship. The Mandak say that "egohup is like minmin," or as one man said, "an egohup is a half-minmin." Just as pavugu is likened to metak in some aspects, so egohup has similarities to the minmin category. Both are cross-sex dyads governed by a normative emphasis on "shame," with restrictions on physical-social interaction. A person should not speak directly to egohup or touch or come physically close to him/her, or speak egohup's personal names. Minmin and egohup contrast, however, in that food-giving is of symbolic importance to the former but is avoided between the latter. No food should be given or received between egohups, since they do not belong to the same maternal nurture units within which sharing is emphasized. In contrast to nimugu, egohup does not participate in extending paternal substance by ritual food gifts.

Egohups may or may not be in a marriageable relationship. If the moral force of the category is strong, if an egohup belongs to the same ewentus as ego's father or mother's father, marriage between them is forbidden. Marriage is acceptable, however, when the moral force of paternal substance symbols is weak—that is, when egohups belong to social units not connected directly by intermarriage or procreation.

In summary, egohups express elements of paternal substance as a nurture symbolization: they are "like" minmins in the avoidance nature of their cross-sex relationship. Egohup is also a paternal substance relationship which does not share nurture.

Tumbugu/Tumbugu

> *"Evene gabasigia, kakarne nanga, neni*
> *num evene niya ariri tumbugu."*

> "A woman procreated me, nanga of nanga,
> she this woman I call tumbugu."

> *"tumbugu ewenteburubun terak"*

> "tumbugu my ewenteburubun"

Tumbugu stands at the end of a series of social categories. It is a relationship after which a series begins again, often with the addition of *aulit* to the preceding category which "comes back." In this way, tumbugu skirts the outer edges of Mandak nurture relationships. The category may express either paternal substance or maternal nurture symbols, but it communicates these in a more diffuse, less specific fashion than most of the other social categories discussed here. Tumbugu marks secondary, "once-removed" nurture, whether paternal substance or maternal nurture, in which the emphasis on the respective symbols is less direct than in the other categories. The tumbugu dyad may include any sexual combination and members of the same or both moieties.

The Mandak distinguish female tumbugu through nanga and tamak (MM, FM, MMZ, FMZ) as "true" tumbugus, and they are in a maternal nurture relationship to ego. These "true" tumbugus are the nangas of ego's tamaks and nangas and as such represent "second-hand" maternal nurture. The normative role of "true" tumbugus entails the provision of food, care, and sustenance to the reciprocal in the dyad. In this relationship, ego may go at any time to his tumbugu's house and demand food. It is a category within which nurture is shared rather than exchanged. As one man stated:

> The elder tumbugu thinks about her younger tumbugu all the
> time in matters of food. For example, when she finds some
> especially nice piece of food such as a melon, she doesn't eat it
> herself, for she thinks: "I am old and don't need this food, I'll put
> it aside instead to give to my tumbugu."

The Mandak distinguish paternal substance tumbugu, *ewenteburubun*, from "true" tumbugu. This refers to paternal substance tamaks of ego's nangas and tamaks, thus to "once-removed" blood relationships. Ewenteburubun is translated by the Mandak in Neo-Melanesion as *hap-blot* (half-blood), and it incorporates tumbugus who stand in paternal substance relationship to ego's nangas and tamaks. This is the last category with whom a person exchanges nurture through paternal substance. Like "true" tumbugu, ewenteburubun is also a nurturing relationship. However, it contrasts with the former by partaking of the same kind of joking behavior as the nimugu and pavugu categories. Play between ewenteburubuns, however, is expressed in fewer social contexts than that among nimugus and pavugus. While this tempering of joking behavior might be interpreted as due to relationships involving substantial age differences between tumbugus, I suggest that it expresses the weakening of paternal substance indebtedness.

The occasions on which ewenteburubun tumbugus joke are commonly contexts of "first instance." When a man with a new canoe first catches a shark, his ewenteburubun tumbugu may come with knife, ax, stone, or other weapon and attempt to wreck the vessel as it comes to shore. Such attacks are warded off by a small payment of money given to tumbugu by the canoe's owner. The first time male ego marries, his ewenteburubun tumbugu, along with his pavugu, has plunder rights to anything in ego's house. This is another example, therefore, of the same kind of normative relationship as for pavugu and nimugu. Some of the Mandak commented on the motive of tumbugu joking behavior as: "one of his [tumbugu's] Big Men made me come up." Such comments refer not to genealogical relationships but rather to symbolic ties of paternal substance between social units.

Along with "true" tumbugu, ewenteburubun stands in a nurture relationship to ego, in which food, care, and sustenance are given in the direction of the nurturing bond. As in the contrast between tamak and nanga, a difference may be noted in the way nurture is extended in the maternal nurture and paternal substance tumbugu categories. The former accords with the nanga relationship in which nurture is passed "without comment," for it forms part of a person's shared sustenance within social unit boundaries. The latter, however, may receive the same emphatic comment as in the tamak relationship, since both create a debt which must be exchanged against. For example, an elderly tumbugu who doted on his daughters' children and had given them much wealth in land and food complained to me that these tumbugus and his daughters were like "flying foxes" in their greed to consume his food and wealth. Yet his wife did not complain in this manner, for the nurture she passed on to her tumbugus and daughters was shared within maternal nurture units.

Land forms part of the nurture which ewenteburubuns may give to their reciprocals. At a person's death, his ewenteburubun may *soson* for rights to part of the deceased's land. Soson may take place only at the *ekarambis* feast (chapter 5) and involves a payment of money and/or traditional shell valuables by the ewenteburubun to his/her tumbugu's ewentus. Later someone in this ewentus will mark off a plot of ground which henceforth belongs to those who made the payment. Soson marks the last time a person may claim land from these paternal substance connections.

The Web of Nurture

The social categories just discussed do not represent "kinship" categories in the traditional sense in which "kinship" has been defined or implicitly treated in anthropology—that is, as revolving around a genealogical framework.[3] The relationships considered here, whether they are referred to as "kinship" or "social" categories, are forms through which the Mandak create, share, and communicate their symbolic social distinctions. Tumbugu, for example, is not a category of ancestors, but one of diffuse nurture. Mandak social distinctions are concerned neither with descent lines nor with the "source" of nurturing. More important are the contrasting and complementary bonds of nurture, through which individuals differentiate those who share from those who exchange.

In this discussion of nurture relationships, two major categorical distinctions have been suggested in the expressions of paternal substance and maternal nurture symbols. However, all of the categories considered are communicating the focal symbol of nurture, the metaphorization of social relationships by conjoining the provision of sustenance, protection, and wealth with initiation and support of person and social unit.

Among the social categories just examined, male ego derives from nanga a kind of nurture which is shared with a series of other categories of those who receive maternal nurture from the same female source: metak, minmin, the minmin of nanga (tata), and minmin's children (tatas). Male ego is also nurtured by tamak, but this establishes a debt which must be repaid and of which he is reminded by nimugu, pavugu, and tumbugu (ewenteburubun). Through marriage, ego establishes affinal nurture relationships in which nurture is exchanged with his spouse and her social unit, which also includes his emandak-enek.

In this constellation of interrelationships, female ego shares maternal nurture with nanga, minmin, metak, emandak, and ewenteburubun tumbugu. Tumbugu stands at the margins of both maternal nurture and paternal substance and may be defined essentially as a bilateral nurture relationship which reflects either paternal substance or maternal nurture in a diffuse manner.

Among these categories, male and female emphasize different functions of nurture. Female categories, nanga and minmin, are food-givers to emandak-enek and male minmin respectively. The normative roles of both nanga and female minmin involve rituals focusing on the provision of sustenance. Nimugu, as minmin of tamak, acts as a kind of guardian or ritual reminder of the debts created by passage of food from her social unit to ego's.

While females nourish the "other" in dyadic relationships, males emphasize cross-unit exchanging, either "on behalf of" or within a category. Both tamak and male minmin perform important exchanging roles: the former through the prestation of substance and nurture across unit boundaries, the latter in exchanges on behalf of his female minmin with her spouse's social unit. Tata, as minmin of nanga, is a maternal nurture category with a normative focus on sharing, but no ritualization of food-giving. Thus, among the three male/female sibling units, nimugu-tamak, nanga-tata, ego-minmin, the female's role centers on providing food and sharing, while her male counterpart emphasizes exchanging.

In consideration of the sexual dichotomy and the reciprocal actions expected of each (female-sharing/male-exchanging), nimugu and tamak roles suggest an inversion of this symbolic contrast. Although at one level of expression nimugu "gives food" to her minmin's children, particularly in her public food presentations, nimugu also communicates the male exchanging identification. This occurs when nimugu "plunders" her minmin's children's possessions and engages them in joking interactions and when she points out (as she often does in public rituals) the appearance of the "face," "skin," "blood" (physical substance) of her clan in her minmin's children. In contrast, tamak appears to enact "female" sharing with his emandak-enek. Although tamak initiates the indebtedness of his offspring to his social unit by nurturing them, his role is always a "giving" relationship not dissimilar in outward appearance to that of nanga and emandak-enek. Thus tamak himself does not "remind" his offspring of the debt he creates between them and his social unit; rather he *extends* his unit's sharing to his offspring. It is his minmin, nimugu, who manifests a public awareness of the exchanging, paternal substance nature of the relationship between her social unit and that of her minmin's children.

Each of the social categories discussed in this chapter depends for its full signification on interrelationships with certain other categories. The distinction communicated by one relationship is incomplete without its contrasting and/or complementary differentiation in another relationship. The tamak/nimugu inversion of female-sharing and male-exchanging is one example of this interdependence between categories for communication of cultural meaning. Another example is seen in the minmin category—male and female who share maternal nurture. This relationship expresses symbolic meaning in part through a series of other categories, particularly that of *ermasik* (male siblings-in-law). A definitive feature of male minmin's role is to exchange *for* his female minmin. By exchanging with his minmin's spouse and the latter's metaks, male ego validates maternal nurture sharing between himself and his minmin, for such exchanging defines her reciprocal affinal interactions as different in quality from her sharing of nurture with her minmin. Such exchanging also, of course, distinguishes maternal nurture sharing as an exclusive social unit symbol. The Mandak engage in a series of mutually interdependent social relationships, with the expression of symbolic elements in one category embedded with an opposition or complement stated in another category.

The interlocking nature of Mandak nurture categories is an expression of the cultural logic of nurture distinctions and an integrative force in actual social groups. On the one hand, the social categories define and interrelate the Mandak social units of moiety, ebibinet, and ewentus. Nanga/emandak, nanga/enek, metak/metak, minmin/minmin, tata/tata, and tumbugu/tumbugu communicate "being of one kind" through the sharing of female nurture. Tamak/emandak, tamak/enek, nimugu/nimugu, pavugu/pavugu, egohup/egohup, and ewenteburubun tumbugus express "being of different kind" through exchanging of male nurture. Constellations of these two distinctions are the manifest forms of the social units and their interrelationships. Thus in certain contexts which will be discussed in the next chapter, moieties *are* female sharing units which interact in cross-unit male exchanging, and maternal nurture/paternal substance constitutes the dialectic of the Mandak dual organization.

While the Mandak social categories in their symbolic expressions define and articulate the organization of social units, the interrelationships between these expressive cultural metaphors work against actual disintegration of social units. Although space does not permit a detailed discussion of factional disputes, the quarrels I witnessed were resolved most often through the inextricable nature of interlocking bonds of nurture. For example, a quarrel between two women (a man's wife and his minmin), was resolved because both, being loyal to the man (husband of one, minmin of the other), had to cooperate unless they were to disrupt interactions between a number of households. In another example, a quarrel between a man and his daughter's husband was ended because of ties with the intervening woman, wife to one, daughter to the other, and because of a series of complicated nurturing relationships which neither could repudiate without becoming disengaged from a vast network of social relationships. This does not mean that all quarrels are resolved peacefully, but it suggests that the interlocking nature of nurturing relationships works against fissions in the village. Each of the social units—moiety, clan, subclan, sub-subclan—can never be isolated, since each depends on cross-unit bonds for growth and continuation; and a series of social categories, mutually interdependent for full symbolic expression, cross the various social units in a number of directions.

    The Sexual Dichotomy

A Cultural Dichotomy

The sexual dichotomy is a major cultural distinction in most Melanesian societies. Since male/female differentiations figure significantly in the symbols which delineate and dissect the Mandak social world, in this chapter I will focus on the dichotomy's cultural ramifications which are particularly relevant to social symbolizations. In regard to the nurture symbols, female is associated with maternal nurture, social unit identity, and the sharing of food and wealth, while male is conjoined with paternal substance, cross-unit relationships, and the exchanging of food and wealth. Male and female nurture are perhaps the most elaborated differentiations of Mandak culture. The sexual dichotomy epitomizes the dialectical means through which these central New Irelanders create their social relationships. "Male" and "female" are focal elements embedded in complex symbolizations which divide between the two sexes vast areas of the Mandak cultural world.

It is necessary to understand that the sexual dichotomy as discussed here is a cultural division: while there are areas, things, and concepts delegated as "female" or "male," both men and women as individuals may participate in sexually defined cultural domains. For example, although women are instrumental in creating the maternal nurture symbolization—in their roles as nanga, minmin, and metak, and in feeding and nurturing actions—both men and women are members of maternal nurture social units. A Mandak man, therefore, is a member of the "female" social units, moiety, ebibinet, ewentus, in which he shares nurture—a "female" reciprocal interaction—yet the Mandak man also is a communicant of "male" nurture through his roles as tamak and minmin, in exchanging, and in other actions.

Male and female are both distinctions of the focal symbol, nurture. Each sex is differentiated by extending symbolizations in directions which exclude the opposite sex. But such exclusions also contribute to complementing the sexes as co-contributors of nurture. Contrasts which "separate," together with interrelated functions which "complete" nurture, are central themes in the Mandak cultural elaboration of the sexual dichotomy.

In this chapter I will discuss some contexts in which the Mandak elaborate and extend their male and female concepts. The sexes are differentiated in activity spheres, division of labor, food, living areas, and environmental domains. Certain social categories will be considered further in relation to sexual distinctions; and relationships which express the affinal nurture symbol will be discussed.

Taro and Fish

The female side of the sexual dichotomy is associated with taro, culturally the most important of Mandak foods. As one woman stated in a Neo-Melanesian metaphor, *"Taro em i bon bilong kontri"* ("taro is bone of our country"). No feast is complete without it, and, as mentioned earlier, the Mandak begin and end their lives in association with this tuber.

According to the Mandak, a culture heroine named Sigidigum discovered taro and gave it to their ancestors. It is said that Sigidigum found the first taro plant in the bush and planted it behind her house. To make it grow, she performed the taro magic which is still used today. After the taro multiplied, she distributed the tubers among all ebibinets. Each social unit gave a different color to their taro to produce the multiple varieties grown today.

Derived from a woman, taro continues to be the province of females. Men are responsible for the heavy slash-and-burn work of preparing new gardens, but the planting, weeding, and harvesting of taro is women's work. Its preparation and cooking are also *"wok bilong ol meri"* and the shell knife, *egelas*, used to cut and scrape taro is exclusively female property. Knowledge of taro varieties, names, and forms is part of a woman's cultural inheritance. Naming taro types for me was one of the few instances in which men always deferred to the opposite sex. Although women are not the major practitioners of magic, women as well as men perform the special words and gestures which make taro grow well, which make its leaves "spread wide as the wings of Emalam [eagle]." Taro magic is said to be the only context in which a woman may use the powerful *ewasop*, ginger plant, which figures importantly in much of Mandak magic.

In a cultural sense taro is a female plant, although its sustenance is valuable to both sexes. Only a woman may be given a taro name for her personal name, often that of a taro variety belonging to her own ebibinet. Persons in an avoidance relationship to someone with a taro name—for example, minmin, or egohup—must avoid mentioning, handling, or eating that variety.

Vegetable foods are associated generally with the female side of the division of labor and contrast with the sea-oriented male sphere. Particular vegetable species other than taro, however, such as sweet potatoes, beans, and leafy vegetables, are not conceptually female. Bananas do not appear to be involved in the sexual dichotomy, although they usually fall into the realm of men's work. One man provided a sexual classification of some forty to fifty varieties of bananas, but no one else agreed or had heard of male and female banana types.

The sea is a male activity domain. Although men spend a considerable portion of their actual time in heavy garden work, conceptually the sea and its inhabitants are male areas, in contrast to female-taro-gardening associations. Men complain today that more and more of their energies must be diverted from fishing, especially to the production of copra and cocoa. In former times, four or five weeks a year were set aside during which men devoted themselves exclusively to fishing. During these periods men could not do garden work or eat taro, although women continued to provide them with other vegetable foods. Today these intensive fishing occasions are no longer observed.

Mandak men procure and care for all fishing equipment: nets, hooks, lines, spears, and canoes. Making fishing nets and canoes is the prerogative of older men, although today some manufactured nets are purchased in Kavieng. Fishing equipment is stored in the men's houses, and canoes are kept on adjoining beaches. In the past, when larger canoes were constructed, special shelters were built for them on beaches adjacent to men's houses. Finally, fishing magic is always performed by men, never by women.

Just as a woman may receive a taro name, a man's personal name may be that of a type of fish, or an aspect of fishing. For example, personal names in use today include: Damat, "blood of the fish"; Ulibeve, "shark-catching magic"; and Luttam, after a small unseen person who gave a form of fishing magic to the Mandak. A woman in an avoidance relationship to a man with a fish name must not eat that variety of fish. Substitute terms are shared by individuals who cannot say a certain word because it is the personal name of someone in an avoidance relationship.

In general terms, the opposition of female-vegetable versus male-meat seems relevant to the Mandak. However, although men take charge of killing and cooking pigs at feasts and hunt wild animals in the bush, these activities are not conceptually part of male cultural symbolizations. Pigs are not identified with either sex, but are a form of wealth used in exchanges. The fat of cooked pig is regarded as particularly "strong" and is consumed only by men with prestige and political influence. This distinction, however, lies in the realm of association of male with powerful things and does not relate to food-sex dichotomies.

Two exceptions to the male-sea and female-garden opposition occur in the Mandak treatment of seaweed and coconuts. A female identification with the sea is suggested by seaweed, which is said to increase a woman's fertility and general health. While men may eat this plant, it is always gathered by women and is considered a female food. Around Pinikindu certain areas within the reef are known for an abundance of seaweed. A particularly fertile place is close to Lawatbura village. Whenever Pinikindu women attend a feast there, they spend the first few hours out on the reef gathering and eating seaweed. In one sense this plant represents a female association with the sea, while from another viewpoint it might be considered a vegetable that grows in the sea and hence in accord with the female-garden/male-sea distinction.

A second inversion is the conceptual association of male and coconut. Several Mandak related a myth about the origin of the coconut. The following is a synthesis of multiple accounts.

A long time ago there were no coconut trees in central New Ireland. There was a man living in Katendan village whose name was Solala [alternate name, Songalarala]. He never did any work. Instead, he knew a kind of magic to catch sardines. Every day he would get his net, catch sardines, and then trade them to women for taro. The other men of Katendan were angry that this man never did any work. So one day Solala decided to leave the village. He goes to the first mountain, but looking back he can still see Katendan. So he goes further, up to the far side of Lelet where he can't see Katendan anymore. He builds a house, plants gardens, and marries a woman who lives nearby. He prospers, his gardens grow well, and his wife has two sons. The sons grow up. One day Solala becomes ill. He tells his sons that when he dies they must bury him in a certain place and then keep watch over the grave. He dies and they bury him. His sons watch the grave and out of the place where Solala's head is buried grows a coconut tree. Soon the coconut tree is full-grown and produces nuts. The nuts mature and fall down. But the sons don't know what to do with them. Finally, they break them open and give them to the dogs. The dogs eat the coconut meat and the next day are still well, so the sons also eat some of the coconut flesh. They like it. Solala had told them to give the coconuts one to each village around them and along the coast, except not to Katendan. In this way, the coconut was given to all in the area, although Katendan received its coconuts last, indirectly from other villages. The coconut is thus referred to as "*ewatlik tene* Solala," head of Solala.

A part of the euli death feast rituals of the past was the exhumation of the skull of a deceased man being honored by the ceremonies. The skull was reburied in a specially prepared hole within a men's house enclosure, along with shell money, various foods, and a coconut. The coconut would subsequently sprout "out of the head of a man," thus reiterating the origin myth. The fruit of such trees was taboo to all females. A number of ancient coconut trees towering above the lesser vegetation of Cape Pinikindu bear witness to this custom of the past.

Coconuts were not plentiful until Europeans introduced copra marketing in the area. Older men remember the care and anticipation with which the precious nuts were removed from the trees. In former days, Mandak accounts suggest that coconuts occupied an important position in food exchange rituals, such as between subclans of a betrothed couple and between maternal and paternal social units in the celebration of a couple's first child. On these occasions, small exchanges of both taro and coconuts were reciprocated between subclans involved in the betrothal or birth. Perhaps these expressed the symbolic association of male (coconut) and female (taro) elements in contexts focusing on the present or future conjunction of social units as maternal nurture and paternal substance. It is not plausible to do more than suggest this interpretation since today coconuts are an important commercial crop and are no longer important in ritual exchanges.

Ekolonu and Eantuing

Spatial Patterns

Male/female distinctions figure in the Mandak conceptualization of spatial domains. Within the hamlet, the sexes are represented by separate complexes: the *eantuing*, the men's house with an adjacent enclosed yard, and the *ekolonu*, the women's and children's cluster of houses with a surrounding living area.

Eantuing refers to both the men's house and an adjoining yard enclosed by a dry stone wall. All the men's houses I saw were rather small bamboo-walled rectangles of one or two rooms, with sago-thatched roofs, built directly on the ground. Within the memory of elderly males, Mandak men's houses have always been built in this form and have not been subject to the same architectural innovations observed in ekolonu houses. Before Western contact, all men and boys slept and ate in the eantuing. It was highly insulting to say of a man, "He is one who eats in the ekolonu." Fish, especially, was always consumed by men in the eantuing. Today, although the men's house is still important, separation of the sexes for sleeping and eating is no longer the strict rule. The elderly, single, divorced, visiting, and particularly conservative married men continue to sleep in the men's houses. Except during special ritual or social occasions, however, most married men now sleep with their wives and children in ekolonu houses. Eating arrangements are more varied. Men often have their daily meals in the ekolonu, but when visiting males arrive, they usually retire to eat in the eantuing. On all feast occasions the sexes separate. However, even when families eat together they do not follow Western style, for generally a man and his children are served by his wife, who eats her own portion while she is carrying and preparing food. One of the first Mandak reactions to our presence was expressed by a woman who was surprised that my husband and I regularly ate together.

The eantuing is still an important social area for men. It is the place where men go to do specialized craft work, to make nets, *Trochus*-shell arm bracelets, and *Tridacna*-shell pendants, and to polish shell money. It is to the eantuing beach or yard that men retreat in the late afternoons to smoke, chew betel, and gossip. Before any feast, men meet at the eantuing to discuss and organize the future event. One man stated the matter in the following terms.

> The eantuing is the source of all important things, like *malanggans, eulis*, large death feasts, for it is the place where men think and plan such affairs. Without an eantuing, how can big things come up?

In the past, women were excluded from the eantuing at all times. During special ritual occasions, females were not allowed to approach the men's house area or to speak in its vicinity. Today, however, women occasionally walk through a men's house yard on their way to bathe in the sea, or a few will sit with their husbands on an eantuing beach in the afternoon. Degrees of strictness in excluding women from the men's area vary from hamlet to hamlet. Generally, women are still seen only infrequently around a men's house and never within the eantuing enclosure during a feast. On these occasions I too was relegated to the ekolonu. Cleaning and sweeping the eantuing yard are male tasks; so except for bringing prepared food there are few occasions for women to enter the men's area.

The ekolonu is the part of a hamlet which contains houses where traditionally only women and children ate and slept. Conceptually, ekolonu is associated with female, as opposed to the male eantuing. In the *euli* ceremonies of the past, men were said to receive "names of the eantuing," while women were given "names of the ekolonu." On all ceremonial feasting occasions the sexes separate, women to the ekolonu, men to the eantuing. When a person dies, this spatial-sexual division is maintained in eating and sleeping throughout the mourning period.

In 1970–71, each of the twenty-four hamlets of Pinikindu contained from one to six ekolonu houses. These display variations in style and building materials not found in the eantuings. Some houses are set off the ground on piles, and a few have galvanized iron roofs. Both the roof and walls of one house were of galvanized iron, and another house was being constructed with a concrete floor. After World War II, the Australian government required that all dwellings be built off the ground, but now that this law is no longer in effect many people are rebuilding houses directly on the ground as was done in the past. There is a clearing between the houses of the ekolonu, a space defined visually by low sandy mounds of refuse accumulated along its perimeters from daily sweeping of the central living space. Within this cleared area women execute their special crafts, producing baskets and sleeping mats, and prepare meals. Each ekolonu contains one or more stone "ovens," piles of stones in which the major subsistence fare is baked. Occasionally men roast fish over coconut husk fires in the eantuing. Special fish catches, especially of particular kinds of large fish such as shark, are prepared and cooked in the eantuing, and portions are sometimes distributed later to the women and children in the ekolonu.

Today, the ekolonu is also the site of Western-derived business activities. It is in this area of the hamlet that one may find a copra-drying shed, a male-managed small trade store (located within a sleeping house), a truck, bicycles, and other business-oriented equipment.

Towakogogaga eantuing, Minim clan. Photograph by Berle Clay.

Mogolomen polishing shell valuables to exchange at his wife's death feast. Photograph by Berle Clay.

Men tying taro bundle for stone "oven" at ekarambis feast.
Photograph by Berle Clay.

Mumusim at eruruma feast for her mother; Katentangala hamlet.

Scene at ekarambis feast; Katentangala hamlet.

Dramatic entrance of women about to make an exchange at an egirimis feast; Penaho hamlet.

A coastal location is preferred for the men's houses, with part of a beach incorporated into the eantuing's enclosed yard or adjacent to it. On certain occasions these adjacent beaches were taboo to females. During the euli ceremonies of the past, any woman seen on the beach close to the euli-eantuing was said to be forced to commit suicide by hanging herself. In the interior of Pinikindu Point are a number of men's houses. Hamlets built away from the coast usually have an informal alliance with a beach residence so that inland peoples have access to the sea for fishing, bathing, and washing. In the past, when the peninsula was more densely populated, some interior hamlets lacked eantuings or had separate men's houses on nearby beaches.

Figure 3 depicts the Mandak conceptual differentiation of spatial domains in terms of the sexual dichotomy. Differentiation in social-spatial symbolic distinctions entails a contrast between male-eantuing-beach-sea and female-ekolonu-garden-bush (fig. 3A). In a wider cultural environment, however, the sexes are united in an opposition between human and nonhuman domains (fig. 3B). Viewed in this manner, the human world includes the hamlet—ekolonu/eantuing, male/female, and cooked food—as the world of the living, surrounded on both bush and coastal sides by nonhuman elements. In the bush are the *erogas* (plural of *egas*), nonhuman beings who are neither seen nor heard except under unusual circumstances. Their world exactly duplicates human society; every person has an egas double who is born when he is born, marries when he marries, and dies when he dies. When people encounter erogas, the meetings are generally harmful and dangerous to the humans. The following story related to me by a man from Pinikindu was typical of the egas stories I heard.

This happened in 1965. An old man of Pinikindu was walking home from a visit one night when he was met by an egas. He didn't get home that night and people of his hamlet began to worry and went looking for him. The next afternoon they found him wandering around in the bush. He didn't have any clothes (laplap) on and there were pieces of wood, as claws, stuck in his nails and also in his mouth. The erogas had done this to the old man to frighten other villagers. The old man said he met the egas, also his wife and children, and they had bought his laplap from him and had given him a sack of money for it, but he had tired of carrying it about in the bush and had dropped it somewhere. He had been eating things in the bush, things uncooked that no man eats. He was very tired and hungry when they found him.

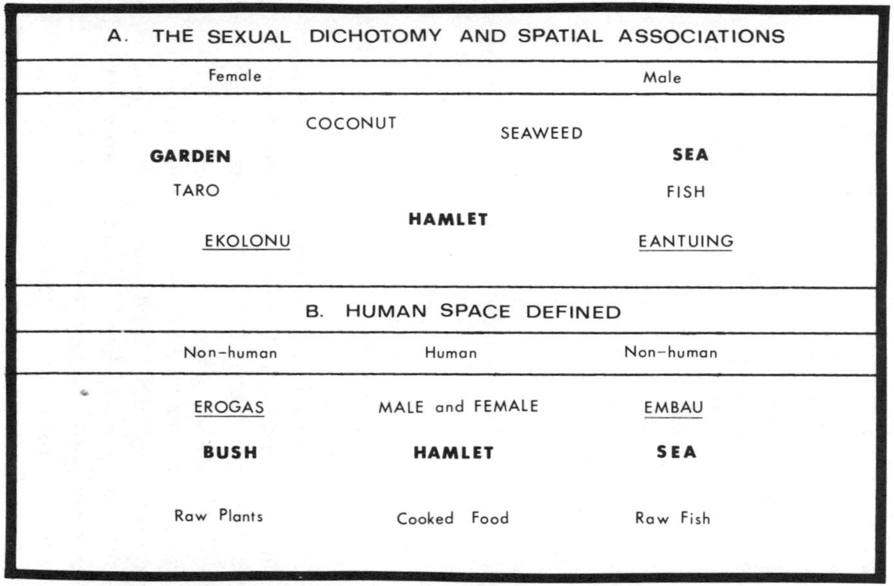

Fig. 3.   Mandak spatial distinctions

People try to avoid egas encounters, therefore, especially by not walking alone in the bush after dusk.

On the sea side of human space is the area of the *embau* (plural of *eu*), the restless spirits of people who died as a result of violence, from sorcery, fights, murder, or accidents. Spirits of those who die from natural causes are called *erogan* and are said to dwell on the small offshore island of Temugu north of Pinikindu. *Embau* spend much of their time at sea, where they eat raw fish. Small rainstorms seen hovering above the water are said to be the embau feeding on schools of fish. These spirits may also roam through the bush, especially at night, and like erogas they are generally dangerous to humans. Embau may kill humans or cause grave illness, and such encounters are most likely to occur at night in the bush or anytime at sea. Embau may also appear to a man when he is asleep to teach him a special genre of dance—*elam, eleplep*—performed at final death feasts.

Nonhuman versus human contrasts are reiterated in the dichotomy of raw versus cooked food. Both erogas and embau eat uncooked foods—wild bush plants for the former, raw fish for the latter. In several Mandak stories, the test whether a newly encountered being is "human" is whether he or she eats cooked or raw foods. The cooked/raw contrast complements the spatial oppositions, with the human world of the hamlet as an area of cooked foods distinguished from the nonhuman areas of sea and bush as the source of uncooked foods.

SOCIAL UNIT IDENTITY

Although the eantuing is symbolically associated with males, it also unites the sexes as a symbolic idiom for the ewentus or ebibinet. The stone walls of the eantuing enclose the burial grounds for both males and females of the social unit that owns the hamlet. A woman may identify herself by saying, "I belong to Katentangala [eantuing]," for it is the place where she will be buried and where the series of death feasts in her honor will be planned and partially executed. Because of population decreases and demographic shifts in clan representation, there are a number of now-defunct eantuings in Pinikindu with which individuals living elsewhere still identify as the "true" place of their social unit. In several cases men asked us to photograph them standing in the places of their "true" eantuings— places covered with jungle growth but identifiable by the remains of eantuing stone walls or ekolonu rubbish mounds.

Each hamlet with its associated eantuing and ekolonu is referred to in popular usage by a single name. Some eantuings or ekolonus, however, also have an additional name. The social unit owning the hamlet generally is known by the name used for both eantuing and ekolonu, except when there has been a recent change in social unit landownership. In most cases, place names have histories too long for people to recall their origin. However, there was one example of a past men's house, Kalambosu, being named after the man, Lambosu, who "bossed" it. Another naming procedure which might be used for a new eantuing is to call it "Katenbanema," after a malanggan death feast has been held there. Today two Katenbanema eantuings are represented in Pinikindu. I was not able to discover naming procedures for ekolonus.

A single eantuing may incorporate an entire ebibinet, a single subclan, or a number of sub-subclans, depending on the size of these social units. Whereas in 1970–71 each Pinikindu hamlet contained only one eantuing, in the past the larger hamlets had two or three men's houses. These represented different social units within an ewentus or ebibinet, or they were built because of factionalism within a social unit and represented the possibility of a new subdivision. The rise, fall, subdivision, and merging of eantuings reflect the history of an ebibinet. Because of the recent low population density among the Mandak, ewentus subdivision is not a current feature. At present it is more common to find a merging of clans or subclans.

The identification of a person with his or her ewentus-eantuing is expressed especially in the events following a death. According to Mandak norms, everyone should be buried in his subclan's eantuing enclosure. I did not learn of any supernatural concepts that supported this norm, but it is obviously politically useful for a social unit to have as many as possible of its deceased within its burial grounds. The prestigious death feasts can be held only at the hamlet site where the deceased is buried. People generally follow the norm unless a strong case can be made for burial in another eantuing. If a person has lived for years in another hamlet or village and there are no members living in his subclan's eantuing, the deceased's affines or blood relations may decide to bury him in their own hamlet. In 1970–71 two cases occurred which illustrate the usual course of events determining burial sites.

A woman of a Turus ewentus died in a Kaluan ewentus hamlet where she lived for forty years after marrying her Kaluan husband. Her spouse tried to persuade people to bury her in his hamlet because she had lived there since her marriage. Although this man was politically powerful and would have liked to control his wife's death feasts by having her buried in his eantuing, he was overruled by general opinion in the village. Several men of the woman's ewentus were living in her Turus hamlet, and they insisted that her body be brought there for burial.

In a second case, a man of another Turus ewentus died in Lawatbura village, where he had lived for most of his life. His mother, born in Pinikindu, had moved to Lawatbura when she married a man of that village. She raised three sons there, all of whom married into Lawatbura. Her own Turus eantuing in Pinikindu lacked residents and had grown into bush. When her son died, Pinikindu men of other Turus subclans argued that he should be buried in his own eantuing. The deceased's metaks and affines of Lawatbura won the case, however, and the man was buried in his residential village. People of Pinikindu declared this wrong, and some, saying the dead man was "being thrown in the road like a dog," refused to attend the burial feast.

The stone wall surrounding the eantuing yard, within which are the men's house and ewentus burial grounds, is called *engas ebolowat*. Engas means "way," "path," "road of"; ebolout is the term of "womb," and *ewat* for "stone." Thus the Mandak expression for the eantuing stone wall, conjoining road-of-womb-rock (*ebolowat* is also the term used for the stone "oven"), reiterates the symbolic conjunction of the eantuing with a maternal nurture unit.

Male Maternal Nurture

From another viewpoint, the eantuing represents a male symbolization of maternal nurture. This feature will be considered more thoroughly in chapter 7 as an example of "symbolic transformation." While Mandak social units are symbolically "female," the eantung provides a context for the male metaphorization of female nurture. There are two basic aspects of this symbolic transformation: certain symbolic idioms associated with "female" and maternal nurture are represented in the exclusively male eantuing context; and within the men's house males express a kind of "ceremonial" nurture analogous to, but different from, the nurture associated with females. Since the former aspect is discussed in chapter 7, I will focus here on the latter.

A recurring pattern in many Mandak ceremonial events expresses the differentiation of the sexes in nurturing roles. In procreative nurture, the male initiates procreation through the prestation of substance, while the female provides continuing, life-sustaining nourishment and protection. This distinction is reiterated in a different form in the Mandak ceremonial sphere. In procreation, a social unit provides substance and nurture for another social unit and receives in return wealth—pigs, shell valuables, or money. In planning and executing death feasts for their ebibinet's deceased, men "initiate" the events through prestations of wealth to other social units, "to make come up" the dances, *malanggans, eulis*, and feasts for their own ebibinet. In both procreation and ceremonies, females provide supportive and continuing sustenance. Thus, although men cannot add to the actual membership of their own clan through procreation, in planning and executing feasts they contribute to its ceremonial growth and honor. I use "ceremonies" loosely to refer to the formal dance and malanggan rituals as well as to feasts, which are only eating and exchanging occasions.

This aspect of Mandak sexual distinctions—nurture derived from females and transformed by males through ceremonial creativity—is reflected in the origin myth of the *wowora* malanggan. The *wowora* is said to have originated from the interior Mandak peoples, possibly around Lelet Plateau.[1] "Wowora" refers to both the malanggan artifact, a large wicker circular object, and the ceremonial complex in which it is involved. Women formerly were never to see or approach this powerful malanggan, a taboo no longer observed. The origin myth of the wowora, as told to me by the Mandak, is as follows.[2]

> A woman was walking home from the gardens one day when it started to rain and she took refuge under a banana plant. She fell asleep, and while she slept the ideas of the wowora complex were given to her in every detail (from whom, no one could say): how to make the malanggan, the accompanying songs and dances. The songs and their accompaniment on the bamboo slit gong were sounded by the rain beating on the leaves sheltering her. When she awoke, she thought: "Why were these things told to me? I am only a woman!" She returned to the village and went to see her minmin, to whom she told the entire complex. Then she went home and hanged herself. Her minmin carried out the first wowora ceremony in her honor at her death feast.

In the Mandak nurture pattern, females sustain the ebibinet and are responsible for its existence through primary and continuing nurture. The deaths of ebibinet members provide the contexts for creative "male" expressions for their own social units. In the wowora myth, the malanggan originates from a woman, just as the ebibinet is derived from "female." However, the wowora is a ceremonial item: it cannot be perpetuated by females but must be "made to come up" within and for the social unit by males. Thus, it is the woman's male minmin who actually plans and executes the first wowora, a ceremony in honor of her death and their ebibinet, an event from which females are excluded as expressive participants. It is the eantuing that provides the context for this kind of male ceremonial nurture.

While men exchange wealth for dance forms and special rituals, these are not retained within ebibinet boundaries but form part of the flow of ceremonial things between social units. Dance forms, the execution of rain, sun, and taro magic are purchased for ebibinet feasts; for each event, rituals should be bought from another social unit. In effect, there must be an exchange of wealth outside the ewentus to make ceremonial things "come up" within it. Thus, males give substance in procreation to other social units, and wealth is returned to the "male" social unit: males also give wealth to other clans to initiate and sustain ceremonial things for their own clans. In this way, the eantuing is a context for the male metaphorization of maternal nurture as ceremonial creativity.

SEPARATION OF THE SEXES

Situational Avoidance

The sexual dichotomy forms a major distinction of the Mandak nurture symbols. The differences between male and female are elaborated by diverse expressions in multiple contexts. With so much emphasis on sexual contrasts, it is not surprising that the Mandak also surround the interaction of men and women with numerous precautions. In specified circumstances, a person must restrict or altogether avoid interactions with the opposite sex.

At recognized points of an individual's life cycle and during his/her engagement in certain activities, the difference between the sexes is emphasized by prescribed restrictions on male/female interaction. To the Mandak, the sexes are contrasting kinds of persons. Contact between them in some contexts can be inimical to the life or well-being of one or both. The situations governed by restrictions for males predominantly involve special male ceremonial or skill activities. For females, sexual taboos surround their involvement with gestation, birth, and parturition. For both sexes, death in the community produces a segregation of males and females for a period of mourning.

When men are concerned with activities described by the Mandak as "strong" (*evevereng*), they must avoid contact with the opposite sex. In contexts when a man's perception, strength, and skill should be especially acute, he must remove himself from female interactions, which would deplete his physical and mental resources. In precontact days these occasions included warfare, extensive fishing periods, and the euli ceremonial complex. Today the situations in which men must particularly maintain their strength and mental acuity include the preparation and performance of certain dances for final death feasts—for example, *eanis, elam*—and the implementation of "strong" magic—for example, rain-making, shark-catching, and special fishing magic. Men participating in these activities should observe some or all of the following restrictions: (*a*) abstinence from sexual intercourse; (*b*) avoidance of eating with or close to females; (*c*) abstinence from taro cooked inside a stone oven, although *egankayie* or *erouma* taro, cooked on top of stones and only partially scraped, is an acceptable substitute; and (*d*) abstinence from eating fish. This last taboo is said to be a precaution against the embau, whose appetites center on fish.

Females do not participate in special activities which require "strength" when they must be "light" (*ebambalak*) rather than "heavy." They do not handle "powerful" things, the eulis, malanggans, or strong magic. During the preparation and performance of certain female dances (e.g., *eleplep*), participants must abstain from sexual intercourse. Such periods, however, last only two to three weeks, whereas males must avoid sexual contact for two to three months before their own dances. Food taboos for females also contrast with those for males. Women do not abstain from taro cooked inside a stone oven, since taro and the stone oven are female symbolic idioms. However, they should observe restrictions on eating certain varieties of fish, particularly shark, before and during their childbearing years. I did not learn the exact nature of the danger involved in eating these sea products, only that they would cause grave illness or death to a young female or to a woman and her children.

In summary, men abstain from taro cooked in a stone oven; women avoid fish under certain conditions. Each sex thus refrains from consuming certain foods identified symbolically with the opposite sex, men in contexts demanding strength, women during their fertile years. Both sexes abstain from taro during periods of special mourning and both refrain from eating certain varieties of fish if ill health is said by a healer to demand it.

The sexes must avoid certain kinds of interactions during recognized periods of the life cycle. A woman should not have sexual intercourse during pregnancy or for about one and a half years afterward, while she is nursing. In former days, an infant was not to be touched during the first three months of life by young adults of either sex other than the parents, since such people, being sexually active, were likely to contaminate the baby's health in some unspecified way. This precaution is no longer observed.

After a death a period of sexual abstinence should be observed by those who participate in mourning. In the past, when a person died men and women of the community would separate to eat and sleep in the dead person's *eantuing* and *ekolonu* for about three months. Today this postmortem segregation lasts for only two to three weeks and involves not the entire village, but usually from ten to fourteen persons related to the deceased in paternal substance, maternal nurture, and affinal nurture relationships of relatively strong moral force.

In summary, interaction between male and female, especially sexual contact, is thought to be debilitating, particularly to the strength of males, and is therefore avoided on occasions when male strength and awareness must be acute. Failure to observe these taboos may result in death because of carelessness in executing the special task, or it may simply cause a faulty, embarrassing performance.

Being involved in fewer special activities than men, females are less subject to cross-sex taboos except during pregnancy, birth, and parturition and when there is a death in the community. It is mainly when a woman's nurturing functions are particularly intense that she should abstain from sexual interaction. For males, it is when they are involved in activities demanding special power or strength that their abilities must not be impaired by sexual contacts.

"Shame" in Social Relationships

In addition to the Mandak focus on sexual separation in certain contexts, cross-sex interactions are also restricted in particular social categories. In discussing these relationships, the Mandak invariably mention the term *emangai,* which they translate into Neo-Melanesian as *sem* ("shame"). The word recalls a complex Mandak concept which has many variations in different contexts.[3] I will mention only certain aspects of "shame" relevant to male/female symbolizations. The word may refer to a person's sensitivity to and embarrassment about immoral actions in a role, relationship, or situation. A person can "have shame" because of a violation of normative prescriptions in a role. The concept may also be involved in descriptions of the "quality" of normative interactions in a category or situation. For example, a common expression about the minmin relationship was: "I have shame toward my minmin." In this expression, a person is not confessing to an immoral act, but is indicating a sensitivity to restrictions on minmin interaction. "Shame" is used to describe certain categories for which normative definitions allow rather limited kinds of interactions between persons in the relationship. In contrast to these "shame" categories are those, such as nimugu, in which the normative role enjoins informality and multiple kinds of behavior. A person cannot have "shame" toward a nimugu.

Two social categories governed by "shame" are minmin and egohup. While the general relationship between the sexes is described by the Mandak as involving "shame," it is the minmin category which epitomizes sexual separation. As was discussed in chapter 3, the minmin category entails two aspects of symbolic sexual differentiation: female sharing and male exchanging. Male and female in the minmin relationship should not speak each other's personal name in address or reference. When conversing, they address each other by the plural form of the personal pronoun to avoid the illusion of intimate interaction. In greeting a minmin, a person says: "How are you (plural)?" A respectful distance should be maintained between them; they must not touch one another or sit or stand within one to two feet of each other. In speaking to a minmin, a person averts his glance rather than looking directly into the other's eyes. One man explained:

> A man must not look at his minmin's eyes or face when he talks to her. Why? Because when a man looks at a woman, he notices the way she has combed her hair or that her face is pretty, and he thinks things no good.

Separation of minmins also entails avoiding each other's personal property. For example, a person should not walk under a clothesline on which his minmin's laplap is hanging or under her house. A person should not touch his minmin's baskets or other possessions.

He must not take food directly from his minmin's hands, although the indirect sharing of food is an important symbolic expression of this relationship.

The minmin relationship emphasizes the prohibition of sexual intercourse, joint procreation, and marriage between those related by maternal nurture, and it provides a distinctive contrast in this way with the *nisok*, husband/wife category. At marriage a man pays his bride's minmin part of the bride-price "to remove the shame," to define the marital union apart from the maternal nurture relationship.

The emphasis in the minmin relationship on sexual separation receives dramatic expression in the traditional response of a man upon hearing a reference made to his minmin's sexuality. In precontact days, a man would respond by causing his minmin's death, by calling her by his own personal name or the name of the *Labakarat* euli, [4] after which she would be compelled to hang herself. The person who spoke publicly of the woman's sexuality would then have to reciprocate with a death in his own ebibinet. Today, however, rather than force death upon his minmin, a man will kill a pig and present it to the publicizer of his minmin's sexuality. The pig must later be reciprocated. This situation appears to assume two different forms. In a violent quarrel, a man may insult another by saying that the latter had intercourse with his own minmin. A dissimilar context involves gossip about a woman's adultery in the presence of her minmin. Only one of these situations, involving the latter form, occurred while I was in Pinikindu. In this case, about ten men were drinking beer one afternoon when one man spoke of an adulterous affair between a Pinikindu man and a woman of another village. The woman was a classificatory minmin, of a different ebibinet, of one of the drinkers. The latter immediately went to spear one of his own pigs, which he then presented to the man who spoke of the woman's affair. [5]

The custom of presenting a pig to an offender is called *egawuk*. It is said to have originated in the seclusion periods which were part of certain male rituals. If one man insulted another during these periods, the offended man would present the other with a pig, which had to be reciprocated later. This custom was adopted for use as a minmin response when the Australian government forbade minmin "murders," or forced suicide. Today, therefore, the expected response is for a man to present a pig to the person who has verbally intruded sexuality into the minmin relationship. As one man commented: "The pig is now the minmin." The presentation of a pig is also a typical Mandak response in numerous contexts in which a relationship of taboo has been violated. The minmin relationship communicates the conjunction of sharing and sexual separation, and the negation of this symbolization calls for a reaction which dramatizes sexual avoidance between minmins.

A woman may use the minmin category to effect avoidance relationships for her own purpose. For example, when a woman quarrels with her husband, she may call out, "Head of my minmin be in this house!" Her home thereafter becomes taboo to her until the curse is lifted. When the quarrel ends, the woman makes a small gift to her minmin to remove his "presence" and henceforth she may return to her house and resume her marital life.

The egohup category also involves a cross-sex relationship within nurture bonds and entails many of the same restrictions as those between minmins—taboos on the use of personal names and avoidance of physical interactions and proximity. However, whereas the passage of food from female to male is an important expression of the minmin category, food is not "shared" between egohups, who communicate their paternal substance relationship by not sharing.

When the moral force of the nurture bond is strong—that is, between egohups of intermarrying subclans—sexual intercourse, joint procreation, and marriage are excluded from the egohup relationship. Should a woman's sexuality be publicized in front of her egohup, as in front of her minmin, the separation of the sexes in the relationship is threatened. This separation is reinstated by a small exchange of wealth from the woman to her egohup, "to remove his shame."

The minmin relationship is a maternal nurture bond which excludes marriage and sexual intercourse. Egohup, a paternal substance category, may or may not be a permissible marital union. Although ego cannot marry an egohup of his/her father's or mother's father's subclans, marriage between egohups of other clans or subclans is allowed. When the moral force of egohup normative ties is weak, therefore, marriage may change the relationship and its entailed restrictions.

UNION OF THE SEXES: MARRIAGE

While the normative relationship between male and female is one of general segregation, the sexes are brought together in the culturally prescribed context of marriage. The "shame" of cross-sex relationships is removed by the husband's paying a bride-price to his wife's minmin, tata, nanga, or other close nurturing categories. Bride-price does not represent a payment for marital services or loss of the female's work for her clan; rather, it makes the distinction between a relationship of sexual intercourse and exchanging in contrast to bonds of sharing and sexual separation.

A marriage initiates a series of new relationships. Some of these were discussed in chapter 3: the metak, nenak, namuna, naak, and nalun categories, which express maternal nurture. Other relationships created by marital alliances are those of "affinal nurture." "Affinal" is used here to refer to categories which are brought about by marriage and express cross-unit symbolizations. They include: *nisok, ermasik, ermasik egohup, nangene, nangene egohup, erulum,* and *inasong.* These categories cross maternal nurture boundaries and entail exchanging rather than sharing.

The Mandak term used in both address and reference for husband and wife is *nisok.* I rarely heard anyone use this, however, since most people address and refer to a spouse by personal name or a general term, such as *eventegin* ("old woman") for wife. The normative features of the nisok category emphasize cooperation and mutual helpfulness between spouses, especially in their main joint labor of procreating, feeding, and caring for their offspring. They should aid one another also in preparing the feasts and ceremonies of their respective social units.

While nisoks are a cooperative nurturing team in procreation, raising children, and general subsistence, the persons in the dyad remain in a distinctly complementary relationship. Nisoks do not form an undifferentiated unit in which cross-sex features are negated, for they occupy separate niches in the sexual dichotomy of their culture. Traditionally, nisoks did not eat, sleep, or work together regularly. They still maintain a degree of separation in these activities both actually and conceptually. They do not share maternal nurture, but cross its boundaries in their relationship. All the work, subsistence, food, and wealth they give one another during married life must ultimately be exchanged against at their deaths.

When a man marries, he pays a bride-price so that he and his wife may cohabit, symbolically apart from and in opposition to his wife's minmin relationship. Along with the normative permission for sexual intimacy in the marital relationship, the husband enters a bond governed by "shame" with his wife's minmin, his *ermasik.* The intervening link in the ermasik category, the woman, stands in an avoidance relation to one, her minmin, and is sexually intimate with the other, her nisok. "Shame" is expressed mainly in the relationship of ego to his wife's minmin rather than in that of ego to his minmin's spouse. A man will say: "I feel 'shame' toward ermasik because I married his minmin." Ermasik (or the Neo-Melanesian *tambu*) is used as a reciprocal form of address and reference, for neither may speak the other's personal name. Both use the plural form of the personal pronoun in reference and address. While a man must not touch the head of his wife's minmin, this is not a reciprocal prohibition. If in the event of a quarrel a man hears something unpleasant about minmin's husband, the latter must give a small payment to his ermasik to remove the "shame" caused by his misconduct. Ermasiks should avoid one another's personal belongings, such as laplaps and baskets, although they can and often do use each other's fishing and hunting gear. A man should not go into or under his wife's minmin's house or ask him for food.

The ermasik category is extended, as *ermasik egohup*, to the husband of male ego's egohup and male ego's wife's egohup. The Mandak explain the "shame" between these persons as, "I married his blood." The brunt of the "shame" is from ego toward wife's egohup. In both ermasik and ermasik egohup relationships, therefore, a man maintains a respectful distance from the males with whom his wife receives nurture from the same source—that is, from wife's minmin and egohup. A woman partakes of procreative nurture with minmin and egohup, both of whom she avoids sexually, while she is in a relationship of sexual intimacy and joint procreativity with her husband. The males interact with the same woman in different ways and their attitudes toward one another are governed by "shame."

The female counterparts of the male affinal avoidance relationships are found in the *nangene* and *nangene egohup* categories. A woman must maintain the same kind of prohibitions as among ermasiks with her husband's minmin and egohup. Nangenes must avoid one another's personal names, must not touch the head of their husband's minmin or egohup or articles in close physical contact with the other. They use the plural personal pronoun in direct or indirect reference to one another. When nangenes quarrel, a man's minmin may show disfavor by putting ash on her face, while her nangene should respond, "to remove the shame," by giving her husband's minmin a small payment.

Other categories initiated through marriage involve varying degrees of "shame." A person feels "shame" toward his wife's mother, his *erulum,* a reciprocal term. No personal names are used between erulums, and they must maintain a respectful distance from one another. They should not be in the same room or sit anywhere close to one another, or walk into or under one another's houses. They also must not accept food from one another's hands, although food can be passed indirectly between erulums.

Another affinal category governed by "shame" is that of *inasong,* the wife of male ego's tata and the children of female ego's husband's minmin. Inasongs also cannot speak each other's names or come close to one another. Both relationships, erulum and inasong, are said not to be as "strong" in regard to "shame" as minmin and egohup. The former are brought about through marriage: if the union dissolves in a divorce, the "shame" of erulum and inasong is also ended. If a man's tata dies, he may marry his tata's wife, his inasong. In contrast, the "shame" of minmin and egohup is more binding; for minmin it is never removed by a change in marital status, and for egohup it can be removed only when the moral force of the category is weak.

At the death of a person in an affinal avoidance relationship— ermasik, nangene, inasong, erulum—ego is said to "have shame" which can be removed only by presenting a pig at one of the deceased's death feasts. Until this is done, the affine must not go into the deceased's burial yard in the eantuing. These pigs are paid for later at another death feast given for the deceased by his ebibinet. Death disturbs these affinal relationships, which are returned to their normative state only by initiating an exchange between the living affinal kin and, symbolically, the deceased. Food provided at a death feast is said to "belong" to the deceased. The "shamed" affines, therefore, also abstain from eating food cooked for the *eruruma* and *ekarambis* death feasts, although they attend these events and eat food which has been cooked separately for them. Affinal contributions at death feasts are discussed further in chapter 5.

In summary, affinal nurture relationships are initiated by a marriage, and they involve obligations to exchange rather than to share food and wealth. They are cross-unit dyads in which the reciprocals are not "of one kind" as are those who share maternal nurture. Affinal nurture categories may be substitutions for previous paternal substance relationships, but never for those of maternal nurture, to which they are opposed in symbolization and meaning.

Affinal nurture categories emphasize cross-sex avoidance and respect, even though the relationship itself may involve same-sex dyads, as in nangene and ermasik. When a Mandak male marries, therefore, he comes into newly permitted sexual intimacy with his wife while entering relationships governed by "shame" with his wife's maternal nurture kin—her nanga and minmin—and paternal substance kin—egohup. His spouse's metaks come into informal, approachable relationships in which cross-sex "shame" is absent. A woman at marriage also assumes a number of "shame"-governed bonds with her husband's minmin, his tata, and his egohup, again with familiarity and cooperation emphasized in relations with her husband's metaks. In the pattern that emerges at marriage the "shame" of cross-sex relationships is abrogated between spouses but is initiated between ego and his/her spouse's same-sex categories of minmin/egohup and opposite-sex maternal nurture categories of male ego's wife's nanga and female ego's husband's tata.

COMPLEMENTARY DISTINCTIONS

In Mandak culture distinctions associated with the sexual dichotomy proliferate. The symbolic concepts of "male" and "female" are extended in multiple directions—in differentiations of space, activities, food, material things, names, and language.[6] The Mandak person communicates these shared symbolizations by acting within the appropriate sexual domain and by doing and expressing "male" or "female" associations. A woman cultivates taro, nurses a baby, prepares food in a stone "oven"; a man fishes, eats and gossips in the men's house, and organizes feasts.

Symbolic elements incorporated within sexual metaphors are not simply the product of sexually exclusive expressions by men or women. Male/female symbolizations are created as complements to one another, both as differences of nurture and as instrumental elements which together enact nurture. Not only does female minmin express sharing by giving food to her male minmin, but her actions also call for a complementary response of extra-unit exchanging by her minmin. The sign that a man accepts a woman as an adopted minmin is when he exchanges for her with her spouse's social unit. Thus male minmin complements the female nurturing actions of his minmin by acting as "male" to her "female" expression, as both define their mutual maternal nurture social unit. Nanga and tamak express complementary distinctions of procreative nurture through supportive and initiatory nurture, respectively.

Through separate but complementary expressions, "male" and "female" together constitute the edifice of a nurturing society.

The sexual distinctions of Mandak culture are created through roles and actions of persons as "male" or "female." The resulting symbolizations, however, encompass concepts much broader than individual differentiation, for they not only apply to the level of person-to-person relationships but are also major distinctions of social-unit definition and interrelationship. Although the Mandak person expresses and creates sexually exclusive symbolizations, these cultural concepts are shared significations which incorporate both sexes or can be expressed by a member of the opposite sex. Maternal nurture, a female symbol, is thus created and expressed at many different levels: a woman as nanga communicates the symbol in her relationship to emandak-enek; both men and women communicate the symbol in sharing actions within ewentus, ebibinet, and moiety; and men in the eantuing create their own metaphorization of maternal nurture. Paternal substance, a male symbol, is expressed at the level of tamak/emandak-enek interaction, but also in cross-unit exchanging relationships by both men and women, and by women exclusively in their symbolization of paternal substance in the egirimis rituals and in aspects of the nimugu category. In certain contexts, therefore, an entire moiety is "female" in an opposing and complementary relationship to the other moiety as "male."

The sexual dichotomy is not a simple distinction of "role playing," but rather a symbolic cultural differentiation which is expressed in numerous contexts at different levels of social interaction. The separation and complementing of "male" and "female" thus both support social life—are instrumental in effecting nurture—and form its major divisions—as distinctions which define and articulate different kinds of nurture.

Sharing and Exchanging

  The prestation of "things" owned or associated with one individual or group to another individual or group may be an important means for creating and expressing social relationships. "Reciprocal interaction" refers to the communication of a social relationship through giving and receiving something separable and transferable. Among the Mandak, as among many tribal, peasant, and other cultures, reciprocal interactions are a highly significant means for expressing symbolic distinctions. Two culturally recognized differences of reciprocal interaction play an important part in the communication of Mandak nurture symbolizations. I refer to these contrasts as "sharing" and "exchanging." Sharing entails interactions in which, through the prestation of things, persons communicate relationships which are "of one kind." Sharing does not engender indebtedness in either of the persons participating. Exchanging, in contrast, is an interaction which expresses "difference" between persons and groups who are giving and receiving things. Exchanging involves a state of indebtedness in one of the reciprocating parties. It is not necessary to "pay back" a person who has given something in a gesture of sharing. In exchanging interactions, however, the recipient of a prestation is indebted to the giver until he reciprocates. Sharing expresses integration; exchanging communicates separation. However, viewed from another level, all reciprocal interactions imply "integration" in the sense of communication of shared symbolizations between the parties giving and receiving.

Sharing and exchanging are distinguishing elements of the Mandak nurture symbols which delineate relationships within and between social units. People express maternal nurture through reciprocal interactions of sharing and communicate paternal substance and affinal nurture through exchanging. Because reciprocal interaction is itself worthy of a lengthy study, I will discuss only the ramifications directly relevant to the symbolizations of nurture. I will first consider the variety of "things" that are shared and exchanged as aspects of nurture, then discuss the contexts of marriage, birth, and death as important occasions evoking expressions of sharing or exchanging.

WHAT CONSTITUTES NURTURE?

"Nurture" is an interpretive symbol of a complex, focal Mandak symbolization. Although I selected the term because of centrality of food and sustenance as idioms of symbolic distinctions, this symbol encompasses a variety of things and actions. This generalized definition of nurture is crucial to the meaning of the symbol, for nurture when thus understood is valuable in explaining Mandak social interactions.

Before discussing the range of meaning governed by the nurture symbol, let me review the Mandak focus on food as an idiom of social distinctions. The Mandak explain many aspects of their social relationships through references to food sharing and exchanging. The beginning of social relationships for each individual revolves around the provision of sustenance. Procreation on the maternal side is viewed in terms of nourishment given to the fetus within the womb and the infant at the breast. Since this first and most necessary food is provided by the mother, social unit membership follows female rather than male procreative nurture sources. Sharing of food continues to be a central symbolic expression of relationships within social units. This is a symbolic idiom, however, and must not be confused with the actuality of eating together. Among the Mandak, males eat together and females eat together; minmins do not actually eat together, yet they symbolically "share food." At any feast, for example, a diverse group of men eat together, although they may not all be "sharing" food in the symbolic sense.

Nurture includes, in addition to food, its source—land and labor. Both garden and hamlet grounds are owned by clans or subclans and constitute part of shared maternal nurture. Nurture, however, is bilateral and associated with procreation by both tamak and nanga. Part of paternal nurture may be in the form of land from tamak's or ewenteburubun's subclans.

Labor is also an aspect of nurture. Exchanges at tamak's death feast are said to pay back his ebibinet for all the work tamak has given to raise emandak-enek, especially the work of providing food. At the death of a married adult, the deceased's affinal ewentus is expected to pay for all the work the deceased performed for his/her spouse's ebibinet.

Nurture may also be wealth, such as shell valuables, Australian money, and pigs—the major items used in formal exchanges. People pass such wealth informally across unit boundaries through paternal substance or affinal nurture relationships, or they exchange it formally to pay off cross-unit nurture debts. For example, when a man needs a pig or shell money for payments at a death or marriage, he may get part or all of the contribution from an ebibinet tata or metak, or from a spouse or someone related as paternal substance. Older informants recalled that in former times shell money was kept solely by ebibinet elders, and younger adults were dependent on them for access to exchange wealth. Today, with cash obtained from copra sales and occasional wage labor, young men and women may also have their own supplies of wealth. Shell money, however, for the most part remains in the hands of older men and women; and older men, as leaders of an ewentus or ebibinet, control the general monetary funds of their social units. Pigs may be owned by persons of either sex and are obtained for exchanges through various nurture networks. For example, if a married woman owns a pig, she or her husband may use it for exchanges. If her husband uses it in an exchange, the pig is simply part of affinal nurture between spouses, a cross-unit nurture which the husband and his ewentus will exchange against at his wife's death feasts. Items of wealth are used to initiate and cancel debts, but their ownership and use are governed by symbolic distinctions in which nurture is shared by maternal nurture relationships and exchanged through paternal substance and affinal nurture categories.

Magic, rituals, and ceremonies may also constitute nurture and may be given to ego by someone of either tamak's or nanga's ebibinet. Although ideally knowledge of magic should be passed within the ebibinet as part of its core of shared wealth, many men receive magic—such as that involved in fishing, net-making, and sorcery—from a tamak. As such this knowledge constitutes paternal nurture and is not paid for at the time of the gift but is included in the general unenumerated debt which emandak-enek must erase at tamak's death feasts.

The Mandak incorporate certain Western-introduced features within the scope of nurture. For example, children attending government or mission schools must pay a tuition. These funds are often provided by the child's tamak as an aspect of paternal substance. While I was in Pinikindu, a schoolteacher returned to the village for a visit from his New Guinea teaching post. At a feast given in his honor, the man made a formal presentation of three hundred dollars to his foster tamak. In a public speech, the young man said that the money was in partial payment for his tamak's work in raising him and especially for his expensive school fees. He did not give money to his foster nanga, since he shared with her in a maternal nurture relationship. Because school fees are a heavy burden to families, they are often mentioned as something which must be repaid by offspring. In the case just mentioned, the teacher was trying to pay off part of his paternal substance obligations earlier than traditionally expected, before the time of tamak's death. Perhaps because of his cash wealth, the young man attempted to ease the sense of his indebtedness by this early payment. The traditional symbolizations are thus being recreated and expressed through new forms in novel contexts. However, the man will still be expected to provide the appropriate exchanges at his foster tamak's death feasts.

Contexts of Exchange

Marriage

In contrast to its treatment in a number of other Melanesian societies, among the Mandak marriage has never been made a cultural focus marked by extensive exchanges or elaborate feasts. Betrothal of a couple, at infancy or as young adults, was traditionally signified by reciprocal exchanges of a few coconuts and cooked taro between the households of the betrothed. Although today children generally are not betrothed, marriages may still be arranged for young adults, past about age fifteen, by the youth's tata, tamak, or elder metak. Such alliances are marked by informal exchanges of taro and other cooked foods between the households of the couple.

No traditional ceremonies mark a new marital union. Instead, a marriage is established informally by a couple simply starting to live together. An important symbolic expression of a new marriage is when the woman starts to cook for her husband. Today, some of the younger couples are instituting small celebrations to accompany church weddings. However, older couples and divorced pairs still make and end marital unions without ceremony or public statement.

In the days before Western contact, both polyandry and polygamy were recognized forms of marriage, although only the wealthy were said to be able to afford plural unions. A woman was limited to two husbands at a time, while a man might have more than two co-wives, although generally two was the maximum. Owing to the long presence of the Christian missions with their monogamous codes, monogamy is now the only recognized and observed type of marriage. Traditionally, both levirate and sororate were preferred second marriages after a spouse's death. Today there is no preference for these choices.

Other than moiety exogamy, the Mandak do not express any preferred or prescribed marriage categories. They do not share their Notsi-speaking neighbors' prescribed MBDD marriages. A few informants said that within the past forty years or so a slight preference has developed for "marrying back" into one's father's ebibinet, in a different ewentus, in efforts to consolidate land claims. Elderly informants say that such a choice is not part of Mandak traditional norms.[1]

While no particular social category is singled out as a desirable marriage union, the Mandak state a definite preference for village endogamy. As I observed in chapter 1, however, only about half of the marriages in Pinikindu in 1970–71 reflected village endogamy. If a marriage has been made out of the village, the Mandak say that one or more of the offspring should marry back into his or her ebibinet's home village. This is important to maintaining both land claims and a general sense of ebibinet membership and identity. For example, a Pinikindu woman married a man of Lemeris village, moved there, and raised three children. A daughter grew up and married again into Lemeris, and when she had her first child she brought it back to Pinikindu for an *egirimis* celebration, a feast honoring the birth of a first child. Although the tata (MB) of this woman resided in Pinikindu in her ewentus's hamlet, many people said that the feast should have been held at Lemeris, or that the infant's mother should have married back into Pinikindu if she wanted to maintain rights to hold such celebrations in her own ewentus's hamlet.

In precontact days, marriage was sealed by a bride-price of *ewakandu* (dogs' teeth necklace) and a few shell valuables given by the groom to his bride's ewentus. Elderly men recalled that about forty years ago they paid in shell valuables the equivalent of seven to ten dollars for a wife. At present, bride-prices have become somewhat inflated and may go as high as fifty dollars, the maximum allowed by Australian law. Among the Mandak, however, there is absent even today the emphasis on bride-price that occurs in areas of the New Guinea Highlands and other parts of Papua New Guinea. Major exchanges are concentrated at death feasts rather than at other stages of a person's life cycle.

The bride-price is given to a representative of the woman's ewentus in an informal, nonpublic presentation, ideally, close to the time when the couple begins to share a household, but actually often only after a year or two of marriage. Whether it is actually paid to a woman's minmin, nanga, tata, or tamak, this exchange is usually distributed among close nurturing relationships of the bride. The bride-price serves two purposes: it removes the minmin "shame" from the marital relationship, and it expresses exchange interactions between the spouses' subclans. Those receiving portions of the bride-price, especially the bride's minmins, are obligated to use the wealth for contributions to death feasts in the groom's ebibinet. Donors of the bride-price, the groom and his ewentus, also assume exchange obligations for future death feasts in the bride's ebibinet. While a marriage remains intact, unbroken by death or divorce, affinally related subclans should contribute to one another's death feasts, because, the Mandak say, the units must demonstrate their appreciation for the work and food passing between them through the marital union. When a woman or someone in her ebibinet dies, her husband should "remember" how much he and his ewentus benefit from his wife's work by making contributions to her clan's death feasts. The same rationale holds for the wife when there is a death in her husband's ebibinet. The men in her ewentus, especially her minmins, must "think about" the work of her husband which has been for their own benefit by making the appropriate death feast contributions of pig, taro, or other foods.

Exchange relations between affinally related maternal nurture units may continue after the death of one of the spouses for the generation in which the marriage was contracted. The primary debt for affinal nurture, however, ends with payments made at the deaths of the spouses. Divorce may terminate affinal exchanges unless the marriage produced offspring who must make cross-unit exchanges for paternal substance at their tamak's death feast.

Although in normative terms bride-price is wealth given by the groom's ewentus to that of the bride, in actuality it is usually the compilation of contributions from the groom's network of close nurture relationships and is distributed among those in nurture relationships to the bride. Thus a tamak may add to the wealth of his emandak's bride-price, or a pavugu contribute to the bride-price of his tamak's tata. In summary, marriage initiates a relationship of exchange between ebibinets. In normative terms, such exchanges are made between the bride's and groom's maternal nurture units, clans or subclans. Contributions to and distributions of these exchanges, whether for bride-price or death feasts, come from people in a variety of nurture relationships to the marital pair.

BIRTH OF *Eruwan*

More important than marriage for Mandak ceremonial observances is the birth of the *eruwan*, a couple's first child. This is celebrated by an egirimis feast given sometime during the child's first year. The egirimis is one of several "first instance" celebrations. For example, special rituals are observed when a man catches his first shark, when a new canoe goes out for the first time, when a new canoe catches its first shark, and at the marriage of a male pavugu. It is not surprising, therefore, that the Mandak celebrate only the birth of the first child, the eruwan, who receives no further ritual attention over other siblings. The birth of this child initiates the union of two subclans in joint procreative nurture of the same offspring. It is an event which begins the passage of nurture across maternal nurture boundaries through paternal substance relationships.

The egirimis is a feast planned and executed mainly by the two subclans of eruwan's tamak and nanga. A number of other possible paternal substance/maternal nurture combinations may also sponsor the celebration. For example, in 1970 a Pinikindu man was planning an egirimis for his daughter's eruwan. The actual subclan that hosts the feast depends partly on the power and political aspirations of eruwan's close male relationships. However, no matter who gives the egirimis it always involves cross-moiety, paternal substance/ maternal nurture oppositions of the first child's ewentus.

The Mandak say that the egirimis is an occasion in which members of eruwan's nanga's and tamak's subclans exchange food. The maternal and paternal subclans are said to "eat one another's food" at this feast, although the food actually derives from a variety of sources and is consumed by all who attend. Egirimis is usually a villagewide affair, and other people related to eruwan through nurture may come from other villages.

A number of ritual acts and exchanges occur at the egirimis. It is the occasion when eruwan's nimugu makes her first public food gifts to her minmin's child. At the beginning of the festivities, nimugu brings two taro plants to eruwan's household. The parents plant this taro, and many years later eruwan is given cuttings from the tuber for his/her own first garden. It is appropriate for the taro to be a variety belonging to nimugu's ebibinet. The Mandak explain this gift as an expression of nimugu's joy over her minmin's first child. This exchange reflects female, maternal nurture, taro, and social-unit symbolic associations and the cross-unit nurture relationship of tamak's ewentus to eruwan. Nimugu, as female, gives taro, associated with maternal nurture, to her minmin's child in a gesture signifiying the beginning of cross-unit nurture from tamak to his emandak or enek. The gift, I suggest, is both an assertion of "shared" nurture and a statement of eruwan's obligation to later exchange against this extension of sharing.

Nimugu-eruwan exchanges at the egirimis serve as a prototype for other nimugu rituals at this time. Any woman of eruwan's paternal or maternal ebibinet may use the occasion to give small gifts of food to her minmin's children, to publicly express the paternal substance relationships of her ebibinet. A common occurrence during an egirimis is the nimugu food-giving ritual described in chapter 3. These small presentations of food from a woman to her minmin's son or daughter are enacted with a degree of mockery on the part of the giver, and appreciative laughter from observers. For example, in one nimugu interaction I witnessed at an egirimis, a woman went to the boundary of the eantuing, where a number of men were feasting, and called loudly for her minmin's sons. When the two men came forward, she presented them with a few cans of food and a bottle of whiskey, to their outward chagrin and the amusement of surrounding observers.

The egirimis is also a time for much raucous public joking between blood relations, again especially in the nimugu category, secondarily between ewenteburubun tumbugus and between pavugus. The play behavior I witnessed on such occasions was always initiated by older women and usually directed toward females, with fewer instances of "play" enacted toward males. Egirimis is said to be a time when "all women play." Joking includes the following kinds of interactions. An elderly woman appears among men sitting on an eantuing beach; she walks among them shouting loudly and throwing ashes on men of the opposite moiety, on her blood kin. A few men try to escape, but most simply sit and acquiesce to being covered with ashes. A group of women preparing taro for an egirimis are interrupted when some of their number start to throw taro peelings on the bare backs of blood relations. Taro skins are said to produce severe itching which can be alleviated only by putting ashes on the afflicted areas. Soon the entire female group begins to throw peelings on members of the opposite moiety. Again, while a group of women are preparing egirimis food, four females appear on a path leading into the hamlet. They are dressed in men's clothes, suggested by European men's shorts, shirts, and hats. These transvestites, attracting much laughter from the women, approach close female relations of the eruwan, singling out particularly the eruwan's mother's mother and mother's mother's sister. These women become the victims and are subjected to much sexual horseplay by these blood "males." The transvestites simulate copulation with their victims, grab their breasts, attempt to pull off their laplaps, and finally throw them bodily into the sea.

Egirimis joking behavior is said to begin in the nimugu relationship but is extended in general cross-moiety interaction so that anyone may "play" with members of the opposite moiety, except persons in an avoidance relationship. During this occasion, therefore, Emalam and Erangam treat one another as blood relations. The Mandak explain nimugu's egirimis joking actions as a sign that she is rejoicing over the birth of her minmin's first child and is reassuring eruwan of his rights to take food from her ebibinet. The egirimis provides, I suggest, a context for the expression of cross-unit procreative relationships—of the passage of nurture across unit boundaries through paternal substance. The sexual play of women, especially that in which blood relations of the eruwan assume male roles, suggests an enactment of cross-unit male procreative roles. This transformation of symbolic sexual associations will be discussed in chapter 7.

Judging from present Mandak attitudes, the egirimis is a popular feast which is being elaborated by many additions. In precontact times, the Mandak egirimis is said to have been much simpler than today and to have centered on the following features: the nimugu taro gift and nimugu joking interactions; a few dances performed mainly by women; a small feast and food distribution of green coconuts and taro plants to all attending subclans. Because of disruptions caused by the Japanese invasion during World War II, however, no egirimises were celebrated by the Mandak from about 1940 to 1961. In 1961 the feast was again held in Pinikindu, and since then it has been growing in complexity and popularity. One egirimis feature which has changed from the past, people indicated, is the infusion of more "play" across moiety lines. Some people claimed that today's emphasis on cross-moiety joking in the egirimis is a Notsi influence. Others observed that the change also has been taken from their own final death feasts or the *lupo* burial feast, which in precontact days involved the kind of cross-moiety "play" now found in egirimis celebrations. In recent years, therefore, there has been a greater concentration of cross-moiety joking in the Mandak egirimis than traditionally, with correspondingly less "play" at final death feasts.

To illustrate the egirimis of the present and its contrast with the simpler traditional celebration, I will describe an egirimis I attended in January 1971 in Pinikindu. In September of 1970, it was announced that Penaho ewentus would host an egirimis during the Christmas holidays for the eruwan of a Penaho man's tata (ZD). The feast was to be held at Penaho hamlet in Pinikindu, although the child, his mother, and his mother's mother lived in a village twenty miles south of Pinikindu. The opposing blood units were not those of eruwan's tamak and nanga, but involved the Penaho ewentus, the sponsor's paternal substance ewentus (his tamak's subclan), and a subclan from Konos village whose women had married men of the sponsor's ebibinet (his own brother and a man in another subclan within Penaho). The latter affinal relationship expressed in this egirimis, and their rather large exchange of gifts with the Penaho subclan, were said to be Notsi customs which were adopted for this celebration. In another Mandak egirimis I attended there were no expressions of affinal nurture relationships in the egirimis, in keeping with the more traditional Mandak celebration.

Two weeks before the egirimis, women belonging to eruwan's moiety began to exercise their plunder rights in the households of their blood relations. This suggests an expression of cross-unit relationships in which eruwan's clan receives nurture from his/her tamak's social unit. Cross-moiety plunder in the opposite direction, from blood to eruwan's ebibinet, occurs on the first day of the egirimis, at which time people of the opposite moiety may go to eruwan's subclan hamlet or gardens to take such food as betel, bananas, taro, and sweet potato. The explanation for the plunder is that eruwan's ebibinet will be taking food from tamak's clan in the future, and so the opposite moiety uses the occasion to retrieve part of its anticipated loss.

The Penaho egirimis of 1971 lasted three days, ending with a major food distribution to representatives of all attending subclans.

The celebration began with a day spent in cooperative food preparation—a time occupied also in much "play." On the second day, dances were put on by representatives, mostly women, of both moieties. Lasting from dusk to dawn, the dances were followed by exchanges between blood and affinal subclans and by general food distribution to all guests. During these three days much food was consumed: quantities of taro, sweet potato, bananas, rice, and canned fish, five sea turtles, three pigs, and a cow. Twenty-five pound sacks of rice and some tins of fish were given by the Penaho ewentus to each unmarried girl of the village, a gift to be reciprocated at each recipient's future egirimis for her first child. Toward the end of the celebration, an exchange was made of food and various trade store items between the Konos subclan and Penaho. This distribution was performed amid much joking and "mock" public speaking by women of the Konos ewentus, while the Penaho subclan reciprocated with briefer replies by several women.[2]

Recent additions and elaborations in Mandak egirimis feasts involve new forms of exchanges, an increase in the quantity of food and gifts distributed, and longer periods of celebration. From a relatively small-scale feast marking the birth of a couple's first child, the egirimis has today become an elaborate celebration with much greater quantities of food and material goods being exchanged. However, the emphasis remains the same. It is an occasion expressing cross-unit aspects of procreative nurture—the ewentus which gained a member in eruwan has also initiated a debt to the paternal substance subclan who has begun to extend its own shared nurture to "grow" eruwan and his/her social unit.

Egiskebot

With the birth of eruwan, paternal substance/maternal nurture interrelationships are expressed not only through the egirimis celebration, but also in *egiskebot*. In the egiskebot ritual, men or women of a person's paternal substance ewentus may come to the household of that person's grown child when he or she has a first child, to demand a small payment of wealth. Egiskebot, therefore, involves exchanges made by eruwan's parents to someone of eruwan's MMF, MFF, FFF, or FMF ewentus. This payment recognizes the end of a series of blood relationships with the birth of eruwan. Ego and his or her ewenteburubun's offspring are not related by paternal substance, and indebtedness for nurture is absent from this relationship.

Since egiskebot always involves an element of surprise, as an unannounced early-morning visit to eruwan's parents, I never actually observed the ritual. The following description was related to me by an egiskebot participant. Kankedek's and Leleang's first child was born in Tuwaram hamlet. One morning at dawn, when eruwan was about three months old, Rangomat, a member of the infant's MMF's ewentus, readied himself for egiskebot. He powdered his face and shoulders with lime, donned a clean laplap, draped vines around his arms, shoulders, and waist, and carrying an ax set out toward Tuwaram. He followed the interhamlet paths in a circuitous route and called loudly as he went: "Anout! Anout! Where are you, Big Man of my ebibinet, where are you?" Anout is the name of the eruwan's MMF, a man who died some years earlier. As Rangomat approached his destination he called out, pointing at the child's house, "Anout, I think I see your face in this house, are you there? Is the face of Anout inside?" He entered the house, sat in its entrance (he was said to be blocking the exit), and said nothing. Kankedek and Leleang meanwhile had heard that Rangomat was coming and had prepared a small payment of shell valuables and money which they silently gave him. Rangomat then shouldered his ax and returned to his own hamlet.

Any person of the subclans of eruwan's MMF, MFF, FFF, or FMF may egiskebot, usually only two or three persons of these social units actually perform the ritual for any one infant. When a woman egiskebots, she generally brings a taro plant for eruwan. Someone may also enact the custom by "stealing" the baby and taking it to his/her house. The parents may get their child back by giving the appropriate payment to the kidnapper. Egiskebot may be interpreted as a claim to "shared" nurture by the ewenteburubun to the offspring of their reciprocals. This demand, however, is paid off and the proposed relationship is not accepted. Egiskebot marks the end of indebtedness to paternal substance subclans beyond the ewenteburubun categories.

Death Feasts

Burial

Death instigates a series of contexts in which the Mandak express major elements of their social symbolizations. Only at the end of a person's life is the full extent of nurture given and received during life affirmed and accumulated "debts" paid off. I will discuss now the usual sequence of feasts, rituals, and exchanges which follows a person's death. While these postmortem events also provide the major contexts for political maneuvers, the latter deserve the attention of a separate study. I will concentrate here only on the normative death exchanges and rituals relevant to expressions of the nurture symbols.

A death is immediately announced by the loud wailing of women. When a person dies, the community divides according to its sexual components: women congregate to eat, cook, mourn, and socialize in the deceased's ekolonu, while men gather in the associated eantuing. This postmortem sexual segregation lasts two to three weeks, although the traditional mourning period is said to have been close to three months. The entire village does not converge on the hamlet of the deceased throughout this time; rather, a group of ten to fourteen persons from varying nurture bonds of the deceased spend the mourning period in the latter's hamlet.

In precontact days, the Mandak buried the dead either within the eantuing yard or at sea. Each coastal eantuing had an offshore area demarcated as its exclusive burial grounds. With stone weights attached to its feet, the corpse was taken by canoe to deep water and allowed to sink to its watery grave. People could not say what factors determined a sea or land interment. Today all are buried on eantuing grounds, usually in a coffin made from an old canoe.

It is the responsibility of blood relationships to prepare the body and to perform all other duties necessary for interment. Ideally, a nimugu should undertake these obligations, although if one is not available, other paternal substance persons may carry out the functions.

When a person dies of old age, a special burial procedure is followed. In precontact days, the corpse would be propped up on a specially constructed platform and surrounded by mounds of taro which were said to be food for the deceased and were not eaten by the living. After a feast, people sang *lupo* songs around the corpse. These songs are said to be joyous because the person died when his or her "work was ended." Following burial the next day, another feast was held. Cross-moiety "play" may occur at this time, in which the moieties treat one another as blood relations. For example, at dawn when the lupo singing has ended, people throw members of the opposite moiety into the sea. Today, a person who dies of old age is buried soon after death, and the lupo celebration is held a week or two later.

Eruruma

Traditionally an *eruruma* feast was held at the time of burial, usually two or three days after a death. Today, because Australian law requires burial within twenty-four hours and because people say they cannot marshal the necessary food resources in such a short time, eruruma occurs two to three weeks after burial. A small feast of rice and canned fish is provided for mourners immediately after a burial.

Eruruma is held at the hamlet where the deceased is buried and may last from one to two days depending on the amount of food available. The sponsors—the dead person's ewentus and persons closely related through paternal substance or affinal nurture—gain more prestige from a two-day than a one-day eruruma. Feast foods include taro, sweet potato, and pig. If it is a two-day event, rice and canned fish are served to people on the first day during preparations for the second day. Bananas are not distributed, in keeping with the past tradition when eruruma was a burial event and bananas could not be readied by placing them in the ground a week before the feast.

Eruruma is usually planned and managed by cooperative efforts of men of the deceased's ebibinet and men of close paternal substance and affinal nurture relationships. The main sponsors are members of the dead person's ewentus, generally men living in the latter's burial eantuing. The first of a series of postmortem exchanges are made at eruruma. On this occasion, affinal nurture relationships of the deceased (ermasik, nangene, erulum, inasong) should remove the "shame" imposed on them by the death. This is done by contributing a pig at one of the death feasts, usually at eruruma. At a subsequent feast, the deceased's ebibinet pays the contributors for the pigs.

Initiation of the exchanges which will be made at the next feast, ekarambis, takes place at eruruma. A person "marks" (*embinou*) another to bring a pig to ekarambis, at which time the former publicly pays the latter for the pig. An embinou is made quite informally at eruruma by handing a shilling to the anticipated pig donor. Traditionally the mark of an embinou was a string of dogs' teeth (ewakandu). A third person, usually a man known for his speaking ability, announces and hands out the embinou shillings. The recipient may refuse the obligation, especially if a previous debt remains outstanding between his subclan and the deceased's and if the relationship is not an affinal nurture or paternal substance bond of strong moral force.

The eruruma feast serves as another context for the expression of affinal nurture or paternal substance indebtedness through joking and "play" behavior between persons of opposite moieties. At this time such joking occurs only to a limited extent, the initiative being on the part of the deceased's moiety. For example, at the eruruma of an Erangam man, women of Erangam might add an inordinate amount of salt to rice being served to a group of Emalam women.

Ekarambis

The second major death feast is ekarambis. It also takes place at the hamlet where the deceased is buried, usually two to three months after a death. Ekarambis may last from one to three days. Again, the longer the feast and the more plentiful the food, the greater the prestige accruing to its sponsors. Foremost among the sponsors are members of the deceased's ewentus or ebibinet, and secondarily persons related to the deceased through paternal substance or affinal nurture. Food for ekarambis includes bananas, taro, sweet potatoes, and pigs. Rice and canned fish are served during prefeast preparations, and betel nuts and peppers are usually distributed among the guests.

Most or all of the pigs at ekarambis are usually brought by those marked by an embinou at eruruma. A member of the deceased's ebibinet, however, may of his own volition contribute a pig if more are needed to feed the guests: usually four or five pigs are considered sufficient. On the second or third day of the feast, after the pigs have been cooked and readied for distribution, speeches announce the pig donors and buyers and a number of public exchanges follow. The first payments are generally to persons who received an embinou at eruruma. While an embinou may be given for a variety of reasons, it serves primarily as a vehicle by which to cancel exchanging debts to the deceased's social unit. When a man dies, his widow and children must pay his ewentus for affinal nurture and paternal substance. One or two of the deceased's children will give an embinou shilling to someone of their father's ewentus. The latter provides a pig for ekarambis, at which time the children pay (*egursay*) the donor in full for the pig provided. It is this payment which terminates the major debt for paternal substance. If a man is survived by both his wife and adult children, the widow's affinal nurture debt is merged with that of her children and she herself does not make a payment. If there are several children, only one or two will actually exchange, but the payment cancels paternal substance debts for the entire sibling group. When a woman dies, her husband and one or more of his ebibinet members buy pigs from her clan members (through embinou-egursay) in order to make retribution for nurture which has passed between the affinally connected social units. While an embinou is therefore given between persons, it represents exchanges between social units, not between individuals. Wealth used in such exchanges generally comes from various sources within a subclan, and when given it is redistributed among members of the recipient's ewentus.

Payments for paternal substance and affinal nurture are usually not the only exchanges evoked through embinous at ekarambis. In order to clarify this complex, I will illustrate the range of such exchanges made at one eruruma-ekarambis series in Pinikindu. Nonobin of Turus ebibinet, Katentangala ewentus, died in 1970. She was survived by her husband, Mogolomen of Kaluan ebibinet, Lamawan ewentus, and four married daughters. At her eruruma, Mogolomen gave an embinou shilling to his youngest daughter, Marwus. For the subsequent ekarambis, Marwus brought a pig valued at seventy dollars, for which she received full payment from her father in shell valuables and money. This exchange represents the main payment by Mogolomen's ewentus to his wife's subclan for the work, food, and wealth—nurture—which had passed from Katentangala to Lamawan during the couple's married life. Marwus distributed the money among her metaks and other ewentus members. Part of the payment was recycled to initiate further exchanges for Nonobin's final death feast—through *eruavalo*, which will be discussed later.

A second embinou at Nonobin's eruruma was given by one of Mogolomen's classificatory tata of Kaluan ebibinet, another ewentus, to a man of Turus ebibinet, Katenbanema ewentus. The explanation for this embinou was that the tata was "remembering" the work Nonobin had contributed to his ebibinet and "all the food he had eaten from her hand." He was thus paying back Nonobin's clan for affinal nurture. A third embinou was given by Mogolomen's classificatory metak of Kaluan ebibinet, another ewentus, to a person of Turus ebibinet, Turus ewentus, for the same reasons as the second embinou.

A fourth embinou was made by Nonobin's classificatory enek, Miyne, Turus ebibinet, Katenbanema ewentus, to someone of Turus ebibinet, Turus ewentus. The reason for this embinou was that

Miyne expected her elderly nanga to die soon and she wanted to ensure a reciprocal contribution from her Turus metaks, Nonobin's daughters, for her nanga's death feast.

In summary, an embinou is given when someone wants to make a payment or contribution to a death feast. An embinou marks the pig donor for ekarambis, at which time the donor is repaid in full. The major reason for an embinou is to make a payment for nurture extended across maternal nurture boundaries through bonds of marriage or procreation. Such payments mark the end of indebtedness for cross-unit nurture, although they do not necessarily mean the end of future contributions to death feasts.

The pig serves as a symbolic expression of exchange relationships between social units. References to a person's indebtedness to the deceased's social unit are made by referring to the pig as the deceased in certain contexts. For example, when a widower pays for a pig, *egursay*, at his wife's ekarambis, it is said, "the man is paying the ebibinet for his wife." When this same pig is being cooked, it is said, for example, "they are cooking the spirit of Nonobin." The meaning of these statements, I suggest, is that affinal nurture obligations are being paid off—the debts are terminated as the pig, the symbolic form of the relationship, is being cooked for consumption.[3]

An embinou shilling can be given only to a person outside the donor's ewentus. The subclan is the largest unit within which an exchange should never take place, for wealth and food are shared by all its members. An embinou may be given within the same ebibinet as a kind of "reciprocal sharing" gesture—to contribute a pig in order that the favor will be reciprocated at a later date. An example of this was the fourth embinou for Nonobin's death. I would not consider such gestures to be true "exchanges" as the term has been used here, since they are not involved in initiating or closing debts of cross-unit nurture. Reciprocal sharing goes on throughout the entire series of death feasts, as rice, canned fish, taro, and sweet potato are provided by members of the same moiety. These acts are expressions of sharing within maternal nurture boundaries.

After embinou-egursay interactions are completed at ekarambis, another form of exchange occurs called *erutuma* or *erumu*. This involves small payments from a shilling up to a dollar to members of the deceased's ewentus from persons of the opposite moiety. These payments are said "to throw out food." Through erumu contributions, a person symbolically expels food received from the deceased during his lifetime and cancels small debts for nurture that has crossed moiety boundaries. Erumu payments are given to persons of the deceased's subclan, usually to those in close maternal nurture relationships to the dead person.

In addition to erumu, another form of exchange at ekarambis is *eruavalo*. A person of the dead person's ebibinet gives part of the money received from egursay to someone of the same moiety as a request to contribute a pig at the final death feast. Eruavalo is another form of marking someone to contribute to a later death feast. The donor makes a nominal contribution (usually two to ten dollars or the equivalent in shell valuables) to the person who is to bring a pig to the final death feast. This person must himself buy the pig and is not repaid by the deceased's ebibinet. The latter is obligated, however, to reciprocate with a similarly priced pig at a final death feast in the contributor's clan. Eruavalo thus starts an exchange obligation of one pig for a final death feast. Once reciprocated, the exchange relationship is terminated. Only those within the deceased's moiety may be marked for eruavalo. It is another example of reciprocal sharing within maternal nurture boundaries.

As was discussed in chapter 3, another payment which may occur at ekarambis is *soson*. Money is given by the deceased's ewenteburu-bun tumbugu (paternal substance) to the former's ewentus for rights to portions of the subclan's land. Soson claims are made only at ekarambis.

An additional form of exchange, *ewawagasi*, has been borrowed recently by the northern Mandak from the southern Mandak area around Penatkin village. One or more of the sponsors of ekarambis ask someone of the same moiety, but a different ebibinet, to bring an ewawagasi to the feast. Ewawagasi consists of varying amounts of small edibles, green coconuts, sugar cane, betel nuts, and peppers. These are brought to ekarambis, centrally displayed, and "bought" by members of the moiety opposite to the donor. Each of the buyers, men, women, and children, places one or two shillings on top of the displayed food. The money is collected by the donor, who later distributes it among his own subclan for their help in assembling the ewawagasi. The food itself, symbolically an exchange between moieties, is handed out to all guests at the feast. The sponsor who called for the contribution must reciprocate with a return ewawagasi at an ekarambis of the donor's clan. Here again food crossing moiety lines is exchanged against, while it is provided by reciprocal sharing within the same moiety.

Final Death Feasts

"Thinking" about a person's death, the Mandak say, is never ended until the final death feast. The ewentus and ebibinet of the deceased must plan and execute some form of death feast which will "stop all talk" about the death. To complete the series appears to be a concern of the living, for nothing is said about what the spirit of the deceased will do if the feasts are not held. The fourth and final feast usually takes place from two to ten years after a death and generally honors several people of the same clan.

A final death feast is sponsored and planned by male members of the ewentus-eantuing where the dead are buried. Since in some cases a person is buried in the eantuing of a paternal substance or affinal subclan, a decedent's final feast may be directed by persons other than his ebibinet members. For example, a Pinikindu man, X, of Kantorango ebibinet, tried to sponsor a final feast in 1970 for a subclan member who had died ten years earlier. X, an elderly man, was one of the last of his ewentus and was anxious to "finish all talk" about his deceased subclan member. The latter was buried at another ebibinet's eantuing, the deceased's blood eantuing, which belonged to Minim clan. The feast, therefore, had to be carried out at a men's house which was under the control of a Minim Big Man, Z. Because of his lack of wealth and political connections, X planned a small death feast, called *"eringtingtongan."* He proceeded with plans for the feast—marshaled appropriate food resources—but said little about the event to Z. Two days before the scheduled feast, Z announced that it could not be held in his eantuing. The eringtingtongan had to be canceled, for X could not hold the event in his own men's house, over "nothing," since the deceased was buried elsewhere. It is for such reasons that it is important to bury a person in his/her subclan's eantuing enclosure. An ewentus cannot properly complete the death feasts for its members unless they are buried in the social unit's own eantuing.

There are many kinds of final death feasts which may end the series. The choice depends on the wealth, political power, and aspirations of the sponsors rather than on the political importance of the deceased. The reason for choosing a particular kind of death feast is not a desire to win favor from the spirits of the dead but rather is an attempt to gain renown and influence among the living. The least prestigious kind of feast is the eringtingtongan which figured in the case just discussed. This feast may be given to honor one or two decedents and generally involves only one or two pigs distributed during a one-day celebration. It is considered derisive to say that a person "is a man of eringtingtongan." A Big Man will boast that he has never sponsored such a feast for his eantuing dead.

While eringtingtongan stands at the lowest end of the prestige scale of final death feasts, there are a variety of styles and types of feast complexes which can accrue esteem for the sponsors. In general, the greater the quantity of food, especially pigs, and the more dances and guests, the more prestige is gained by the sponsors. In precontact times the most powerful of final death feasts was the euli complex. This long ago disappeared from central New Ireland owing to the efforts of the missions and is recalled only in disconnected bits and pieces of ritual recounted by elderly men and by the enduring austere and magnificent euli figures in faraway museums.

The most common form of final death feast today is called by the general term *euga* or *eloqpanga*. This is a large feast which may incorporate a variety of dances, possibly a carved malanggan, and one or more cement tombstones. An euga usually lasts three days, and preparations may begin a year in advance. Those attending may come from forty or fifty different villages.

Within the complex of an euga its sponsors, primarily the decedents' ebibinet members, have many choices of dances, songs, and malanggans. The clan members themselves may sponsor a dance, especially one of the more prestigious traditional forms— such as *elam*, *eleplep*, or *eanis*—or they may ask people from other clans to contribute dances. Both avenues are usually followed to increase the complexity and prestige of the euga. In the first case, the sponsoring ebibinet must buy rights to put on the dance from someone outside their own social unit. Wealth, in the form of shell valuables or money, is given outside the clan to "make come up" the dance or ceremony honoring the ebibinet's dead. In the second case, the deceased's clan asks people of other ebibinets to sponsor a dance and to take responsibility for its purchase, preparation, and organization. Those asked to be patrons are most likely to be related to the sponsoring clan through maternal nurture (in other ebibinets), and also through paternal substance and affinal nurture.

While dances constitute important entertainment, the euga is first and foremost an occasion for feasting. Vast amounts of food are brought in and distributed. The high point is the display and distribution of from thirty to eighty slaughtered and singed pigs. Other foods include taro, sweet potatoes, bananas, rice, and canned fish.

Food for the euga comes from multiple sources. The sponsoring ebibinet usually supplies a few pigs and makes special gardens for the event, but the majority of the food will come from reparations of past gifts and new obligations begun by persons in a wide variety of nurture bonds to the sponsoring clan. It is recalled that at ekarambis, members of the deceased's ewentus marked through eruavalo persons of their same moiety to bring pigs for the final death feast. Some pigs will come from these obligations and from payments of previous eruavalo debts. A person of the same moiety as the sponsoring ebibinet may also contribute a pig without being asked or previously "marked" because the donor's ebibinet is contemplating its own euga in the near future and wants to ensure reciprocal sharing. When the donor's clan gives a final death feast, the recipient's ebibinet must also furnish a pig. This kind of unrequested reciprocity occurs only within the same moiety and is an expression of the sharing idiom of the maternal nurture symbol.

Pig contributions are also given through various cross-unit bonds to the sponsoring ebibinet. As long as a marriage is intact, clans should donate food, work, and wealth to the death feasts of affinally connected ebibinets. This is part of the nurturing exchanges which cross maternal nurture boundaries.

In addition to dance and food contributions for the euga, numerous smaller exchanges are made in preparation for the feast. Special large taro and sweet potato gardens are planted by the sponsoring ebibinet, which hires the services of a rain and taro magician to ensure a bounteous harvest. Good weather for the feast itself must be obtained by paying a man who knows rain and sun magic. At various moments during the period before the euga, small feasts highlight the beginning or end of preparatory stages, such as when it is time to "clear" the grounds of the hamlet, or when the rain and taro magician receives public payment for his services. A month or more before the final death feast, the nightly beating of a wooden slit gong with an accompanying dance (*ebot*), in the hamlet of the euga's sponsors proclaims a growing excitement about the coming event.

A Man's Worth

A Big Man of Pinikindu was discussing what constitutes the "worth" of a man. He concluded that the most important thing in a man's life is to make good feasts. To do this, he continued, is not an easy matter, since "food does not come out of nothing." It comes through hard work, wealth, magic, skill, and knowledge. Thus, a man who can produce a good feast is truly admirable. The production of feasts by men suggests a male counterpart to female nurture. While females make persons and social units grow by providing sustenance—nurture—males express a social metaphor of "group feeding" in the Mandak feasting events. Although women are necessary participants in preparations for feasts—in harvesting and preparing taro and sweet potato—from another Mandak viewpoint men "give" the feasts through their planning, organization, and direction of preparations and the actual distribution of feast foods.

Whereas under certain circumstances a woman may be adopted by another ebibinet through erembeke, men recruit themselves to another clan by demonstrations of exchanging. When a man's ebibinet is declining in numbers, or when he comes from another area and lacks local clan affiliations, he may ally himself to another clan within his own moiety. He does this by continual prestations of wealth—pigs, shell valuables, and money—at the death feasts of his adopted clan. He thereby expresses the male role of exchanging for his adopted maternal nurture unit, and by exchanging against extraunit sharing, he helps define the boundaries of his sharing unit.

A man from Buka has been residing in Pinikindu for some five years. At present he is affiliated with Minim ebibinet, since one of its members calls him "metak" because they were once involved in a cooperative work venture in Rabaul. However, this man from Buka has not yet been fully accepted as a member of Minim ebibinet because he has not contributed sufficient wealth at its death feasts over a long period of time. People say, however, that if he does make a substantial number of payments at Minim feasts he will be accepted as one of its members.

Mogolomen was born into Lamawan ebibinet, Erangam moiety. However, it had dwindled to four members, and so his mother and her two minmins decided to attach themselves to the more numerous Kaluan clan of the same moiety. To do this they made many contributions for ten to fifteen years at Kaluan death feasts. Although their tangential membership in this clan was recognized, it was only the son, Mogolomen, who by continuing these exchanges has been accorded full membership in the Kaluan group.

Not only is membership within a social unit established by making exchanges; relationships to a clan for purposes of sharing maternal nurture are made in this way. By continual exchanges a man may establish claims on lands belonging to another ebibinet of the same moiety. Such a relationship generally develops when an ebibinet is dwindling in number or when a quarrel has factionalized its membership—at such a point the man who seeks sharing advantage steps in and makes the appropriate death feast exchanges. Before land claims are recognized, however, substantial contributions to feasts must continue for many years. To terminate the exchanges prematurely may jeopardize the person's claims to land from a clan which is not his own.

The Meaning of Prestations

Among the Mandak, no standardized value is placed on things given and received as nurture. The appropriateness of things exchanged depends on the context of their prestation, and thus on the social relationships being expressed. This is not to suggest that "just anything" may be exchanged and assumes its value from the particular context, for there are normative expectations about the quality and quantity of things transferred in different contexts. However, the signification of prestations lies in the contexts of their sharing or exchanging. The social relationships and contexts of reciprocal interactions do not take their meaning from an a priori value set on the things being transferred.

In a public exchange signifying the end of a quarrel, two women in a nangene relationship gave each other exactly one dollar. They resumed cooperative interactions with one another through an exchange of money which assumed a meaning relative to the context. Here the prestations become a mutual indemnity for the "shame" incurred by both women.

In another example, a man terminated his debt for his deceased wife's cross-unit nurture by paying seventy dollars to his wife's ewentus at her death feast. The wealth was given to the ewentus for a pig worth that amount which they provided at the ekarambis feast. In this context, the Mandak were not evaluating affinal nurture at seventy dollars. The amount exchanged assumed the equivalence of the deceased's unenumerated cross-unit nurture, so that through his payment the man returned his wife's work, food, and so forth to her social unit and thereby closed his debt. The contextual definition of wealth and its power to effect a social relationship are clearly suggested in the way the Mandak refer to exchanges made at death feasts. As I discussed earlier, in the ekarambis pig exchange, people equate the pig with the spirit of the deceased in terms of exchange interactions. For example, when the widower pays his dead wife's clan for the pig, people say, "he is paying the ebibinet for his wife."

Another example of this contextual meaning of prestations and their use to effect relationships is the erumu exchanges made at ekarambis feasts. In these reciprocal interactions, persons in a cross-moiety relationship to the deceased contribute a few shillings to the deceased's ewentus, "to throw out food," received from the deceased during the latter's lifetime. Here the shillings are defined as "food received," and by these prestations cross-unit nurture is returned. The interaction does not place a monetary value on food given in cross-unit relationships by the deceased.

The significance of exchanging objects—pigs, shell valuables, money—derives from the exchanging contexts. The metaphorical meaning assumed by such objects is used to communicate and change social relationships. Thus relationships between persons or groups may be reiterated or modified by the transfer of wealth which takes on a signification relative to the exchanging context.

A Relative Focus

A set of Mandak symbolizations has been interpreted through a pattern defined by a focal symbol, nurture, which is communicated through the major differentiating symbols of maternal nurture, paternal substance, and affinal nurture. The latter distinctions are expressed through dialectical articulations of male/female and exchanging/sharing. These symbolic contrasts are interrelated as complements to produce and sustain individuals and social units. The meanings communicated through the nurture pattern, however, are not expressed solely in metaphorical extensions and dyadic relationships: significations are also produced through a cultural emphasis on certain modes of symbolic articulation. While these modes may be subtle in expression, involving only a "relative" focus on the nexus of symbolic elements, they contribute an important slant to the total meaning of the symbolic pattern. Thus social groups which share similar cultural distinctions may display different patterns of social interaction because of contrasts in emphasis on symbolic interrelationships. I will explore this aspect of cultural meaning—focus in symbolic articulations—by comparing the Mandak with their northern neighbors, the Notsi-speaking people.

The Notsi and the Mandak

The Notsi are of particular interest to this study because they share a broad range of sociocultural similarities with the Mandak. Two anthropologists have worked among the Notsi: Hortense Powdermaker in 1929–30[1] and Phillip Lewis in 1954 and 1969–70.[2] Unfortunately their studies do not deal directly with the major cultural symbolizations of social relationships: Powdermaker was concerned with kinship and social organization within a typological-functional framework, and Lewis directed his attention to art. The following comparison, therefore, must be viewed as speculative until

data become available that are specific to Notsi social symbolizations.

Data from Powdermaker and Lewis and my own field experience
suggest that the Notsi and Mandak display such sociocultural
similarities as certain terminological and normative definitions of
social categories, organizational units—matrilineal, exogamous,
moieties, clans, and subclans—certain rituals and ceremonies,
major feasts and exchanges organized around deaths, property
inheritance, the giving and receiving of food as a central idiom of
social symbolizations, and many aspects of male/female cultural
distinctions.[3]

Similarities between the Notsi and the Mandak support the
hypothesis that they share basic significations in their major social
distinctions—that to the Notsi the focus of social relationships is
contained in the metaphors of nurture described in this study.
Maternal nurture summarizes symbolizations relevant to Notsi
matrilineality, relating "being of one kind," female, sharing, and
nurturing continuity. Male is associated symbolically with exchanging and cross-unit relationships.

Although the two cultures appear to share a general symbolic
orientation, differences in emphasis are suggested in the articulation
of exchanging and sharing. Although the Notsi, like the Mandak,
express symbolic distinctions to create their focal symbol of nurture,
the two cultures contrast in the way sharing and exchanging are
defined relative to one another. This difference in focus on symbolic
elements is important to the meaning of the respective symbolic
patterns.

Notsi data lend support to the hypothesis that for these people
exchanging is an extensive symbolization which integrates social
units defined by exclusive sharing. In contrast, for the Mandak,
social unit membership results from a differentiation of sharing *by*
exchanging. Thus, while the Notsi exchange to create continuing
interunit alliances, the Mandak exchange to define intraunit from
extraunit nurturing. In both cultures, sharing and exchanging are
articulated in opposition, defining one another through explicit
contrasts and as complementary actions which support the social
continuity of nurture. The focus on mode of articulation is relative
and is a part of each culture's elaboration of a similar symbolic
orientation. This relative emphasis, however, is reflected in numerous contrasts of symbolic expression in the two groups and has
important implications for the ways the societies are integrated.

The Notsi have a preferential marriage system of male ego with

MBDD, FZDD, and female ego with MFZS, MMBS. Male ego calls WM, MBD, FZD by the same term, *korup*, and refers to MBDD, FZDD, and wife as *tumbo*. Female ego calls MFZS, MMBS and husband by the same term, *malis*. They join, therefore, in single categories certain relationships which the Mandak contrast as paternal substance and affinal nurture, with marriage and sexual intercourse excluded from the former but a part of the latter. In contrast, Notsi male procreative nurture merges with affinal nurture, and this is expressed particularly in the relationship of korup and malis/tumbo.[4]

Among the Notsi, exchange is emphasized as a relational rather than an oppositional symbolic expression. Neither Powdermaker nor Lewis mentions that the Notsi pay off nurture debts to male procreative or affinal relationships at death feasts or other occasions or that any sense of indebtedness defines interunit bonds. Both authors, however, do describe many examples of nurture being transmitted between social units. Powdermaker writes that the passing of magic and other property from father to son is not infrequent, although she interprets this as an example of sentiment overcoming clan rule.[5] She describes a case of land transfer from father to son after the latter makes a contribution to his father's death feast. She concludes that such land transfers are unusual, although again this may be a reflection of Powdermaker's support of "clan rule" rather than actual examples.[6] A marriage feast is described in which the bride's father presents a pig and receives payment for it from his wife.[7] Numerous examples are cited of malanggans or masks being purchased by a *mum* (F, FB, etc.) for his *-tsi* (S, BS, etc.).[8] From these reports, it is evident that among the Notsi, nurture in the form of magic, property, or food is exchanged between social units through male procreative and affinal relationships. In contrast to the Mandak, however, among the Notsi such cross-unit transmissions are expressed *as* exchanges at the time of transference. The passage of food, wealth, and skills in Mandak cross-unit relationships usually does not involve immediate reciprocity; rather, prestations through paternal substance or affinal nurture bonds enter a stream of indebtedness which is canceled only at death feasts.

Numerous descriptions of Notsi rituals suggest the articulation of exchanging nurture as a form of alliance between intermarrying clans. The Notsi ritualize and elaborate the events of betrothal and marriage to a greater extent than do the Mandak. A feast is held for an infant at which he or she is said "to eat with" members of the opposite sex in the opposing moiety, particularly with those in the preferred spouse category.[9] The passage of affinal nurture between social units is not initiated anew at marriage as it is among the Mandak, but is part of ongoing alliances and is expressed in the preferred spouse categories of MBDD, FZDD to male ego and MMBS, MFZS to female ego. Before marriage, males give food to their korup's daughters.[10] If a woman marries someone other than the preferred spouse, her husband must pay the latter for the food gifts she already had received from him.[11] Premarital gifts are exchanged against if the alliance is not continuous through marriages.

The emphases suggested for the Notsi and Mandak are reflected in certain contexts in analogous social relationships. Of particular interest because of the interplay between symbolic expressions of the sexual dichotomy, reciprocity, and same-unit/cross-unit are the categories of B/Z (minmin and matonga), H/W (nisok and malis/tumbo), and WM/DH (erulum and korup). Minmin, matonga, erulum, and korup all entail a degree of separation and avoidance between male and female, while they contrast in this respect with the sexual union permitted in the nisok and malis/tumbo relationships. However, the Notsi and the Mandak place noticeably different stresses on sexual separation and the treatment of female sexuality in these relationships.

As I discussed in chapter 4, the Mandak emphasize the exclusion of sexuality in the minmin relationship. Male/female avoidance for the Notsi, however, is most sharply defined in their korup relationship. While the matonga category is said to entail a degree of avoidance within the dyad, Powdermaker writes that classificatory matongas were often seen showing public affection for one another, a form of behavior seemingly condoned rather than forbidden.[12] She also describes the case of an old man who made continual sexual jokes about a woman in the presence of her matonga, and while such behavior was frowned upon, it was tolerated.[13] In contrast, korup is said to be the relationship "surrounded with the most ritual prohibitions."[14]

The contrast between the Notsi and Mandak in regard to emphasis on sexual separation in the korup and minmin relationships accords with their respective modes of articulating sharing and exchanging symbolizations. The Notsi focus on male/female avoidance in the area of cross-unit relationships. The korup category mediates alliance relationships from procreative (FZ, MB) to affinal (FZDD, MBDD). For male ego, korup is a vital maternal nurture link to his preferred spouse, as her *nangga* (M, MZ, etc.). Yet she is also *tsaina* (D, MZD, etc.) to his procreating relationships of FZ and MB. I suggest that avoidance norms are particularly strong in the korup category because it occupies a sensitive area of cross-unit relationships in turning procreative into affinal alliances.

The Mandak focus on the minmin relationship for sexual separation also follows from the category's position among maternal nurture/affinal nurture interrelationships. My previous discussions of erembeke, bride-price, and affinal exchanges have indicated that the Mandak effectively bracket affinal interactions with rituals and expressions which distinguish affinal from procreative nurturing. I suggest that the Mandak emphasize sexual separation in the minmin relationship as a means of excluding cross-unit exchanging from same-unit sharing. Earlier I mentioned the significance the Mandak place on the minmin relationship for a woman: it is male minmin, whose "shame" is separated from the nisok bond through bride-price, who exchanges with his minmin's spouse and excludes affinal nurturing from maternal nurture sharing. The sexual separation of minmin, reiterated in the ermasik and nangene relationships, acts as a symbolic buffer between same-unit/cross-unit interrelationships, allowing a communication of differences.

An additional aspect of the categories just discussed which also appears to support the suggested contrast between the Mandak and Notsi is the treatment of female sexuality, or more particularly, female adultery. For the Notsi, an acceptable procedure in the case of a woman's extramarital affair is for the woman's lover to give her a shell valuable which she later passes on to her husband.[15] As I indicated earlier, the Mandak place a certain degree of "control" of a woman's sexuality in the minmin relationship. Such control is expressed through the bride-price and more dramatically in the custom whereby a man, upon hearing a reference to his minmin's adultery, in the past would cause her death, while today he presents a pig to the publicizer of the adultery. No mention is made of a relationship between a Notsi woman's adultery and her matonga or clan relationships. Among the latter, therefore, because exchanging is an expression of interunit alliances, female adultery becomes the concern of cross-unit relationships. For the Mandak, the legitimate expression of female sexuality must be defined in contrast to a woman's maternal nurture relationships, for it is the differentiation of cross-unit exchanging (and sexual union) from same-unit sharing (and sexual separation) which receives the Mandak focus in symbolic articulations.

Comparisons of other Mandak and Notsi social categories lend support to the hypothesis that exchanging is emphasized as an alliance symbolization by the Notsi but as an oppositional, exclusive symbolization by the Mandak. The categories of *tamangaina* (FZ, FMZD, etc.) and *ripunga/ripungaina* (same-sex cross-cousins, etc.) differ in certain respects from the comparable nimugu and pavugu categories of the Mandak. Remember that both nimugu and pavugu remind persons of their indebtedness to their tamak's social unit for cross-unit nurture. The nimugu and pavugu joking relationships involve ritual gifts and plunder, which state a debtor-creditor inequality. From Powdermaker's descriptions, tamangaina and ripunga/ripungaina are not joking relationships, although discussion of the normative features of these categories is minimal.[16] Tamangaina exchanges appear to be reciprocal. They exchange taro with each other at birth feasts, an act which becomes the model for general cross-moiety taro exchanges between women.[17] At the Mandak egirimis, nimugu gives her minmin's child food gifts, but the latter does not reciprocate. At male circumcision rites, before viewing the malanggans, the circumcised boys present their tamangainas with taro and pigs entrails and receive shell money and tobacco.[18] Taro is an idiom of maternal nurture, so that through this exchange the boys express nurturing continuity *between* social units. Tamangaina's counterprestation of shell money and tobacco defines the "continuity" as exchanging rather than sharing. Among the Mandak this ritual would be reversed, with nimugu giving taro to her minmin's offspring as a claim to "shared" nurture and the latter's indebtedness and obligation to ultimately exchange against nurture derived from her ebibinet.

Complementary and Symmetrical Interactions

Although the Notsi and Mandak appear to share a similar orientation in certain cultural symbolizations, important shifts in modes of symbolic articulation have been suggested. Sharing and exchanging define and relate social units and persons of "like" and "unlike" nurturing constitution in both cultures. Yet among the Mandak persons are related through an apparent "sharing" of nurture as an extensive action, which is dichotomized by exchanging into same-unit sharing versus cross-unit exchanging. While the giving of nurture between social units is always exchanging, it yet presents itself as "sharing," as a metaphor binding persons in the general relationship of nurture. However, for the Notsi the exclusiveness of sharing within units receives relatively less emphasis, while special attention is given to cross-unit exchanging in multiple contexts.

In accordance with these contrasting emphases, the Notsi have constituted their social interrelationships more toward a model of symmetrical nurturing interactions: the Mandak have realized their nurturing orientation along the lines of complementary interrelationships. In emphasizing cross-unit exchange as an ongoing feature of interunit relationships, the Notsi have elaborated their contextual expressions of affinal bonds and incorporated procreative relationships within a generalized cross-unit symbolization. In many contexts, the Notsi moieties engage in mutual exchanges to suggest a symmetrical model of dual organization, each side exchanging with the other, neither in a subordinate debtor relation to the other. In contrast, the Mandak produce a complementary effect in cross-moiety interactions through an emphasis on procreative relationships. The Mandak celebrate the egirimis rather than marriage alliances. In contexts such as the egirimis and certain death-feast rituals, cross-moiety relationships are generalized as "blood." Although in the egirimis mutual exchanging is expressed between Emalam and Erangam—"we eat each other's food"—the predominant tone of the celebration is one of procreative difference between the moieties in a complementary relationship to eruwan and his social unit. At a man's death, the exchanges of his children for paternal substance are larger and more socially important than the exchanges of his spouse for affinal nurture, and the latter may become totally submerged by her offspring's payments. In summary, the Mandak emphasize different contributions to nurture and in this way they relate their social units along complementary lines. The Notsi focus on the integration of sharing units through mutual affinal exchanges and thus present moiety interaction in symmetrical terms.

This symmetrical/complementary contrast is relative within the two cultures, for both the Notsi and the Mandak articulate their nurturing symbolizations in both symmetrical and complementary fashion. It is possible that the presence of both forms in each culture provides a necessary balance in social dynamics along the lines discussed by Bateson.[19]

While at this time I cannot suggest causes for the ways in which the Notsi and Mandak have constituted their nurture symbolizations, it is possible that either culture might move in the direction of the other. For example, should the Mandak begin to concentrate their marital alliances between particular ebibinets and to focus on such alliances of mutual exchanging, it is possible that their social interactions might move toward a symmetrical model. The Mandak have expressed an interest in consolidating land rights by "marrying back" into one's tamak's ebibinet (different ewentus). With increasing importance being placed on marketing coconuts and cacao, the concentration of permanent land rights has obvious advantages. If the Mandak population should increase appreciably in the future, the pressure for land might lead to an increasing interest in marriage alliances between particular clans. It is conceivable, therefore, that a change in population density and patterns of land use could influence a "turning" in relative emphasis on modes of symbolic articulation. Yet such a shift would not be a simple one effected only through a change in marital patterns, for the focus on symbolic interrelationships, relative though it may be, is embedded within symbolizations expressed in numerous forms and multiple contexts.

INVERSION

The Mandak nurture pattern entails a series of complementary and contrasting distinctions through which meaning is expressed in an ongoing dialogue between symbolic elements—male/female, exchanging/sharing, same-unit/cross-unit, sexual separation, sexual union, and so forth. Nurture as a focal symbol is communicated through the articulation of contrasting symbols—maternal nurture, paternal substance, and affinal nurture. These differentiations, however, are not always expressed through extensions of contrast, for in certain contexts the distinctions of nurture appear inverted. These inversions, which I call "symbolic transformations," involve a rearrangement of the usual symbolic associations, so that one symbol or symbolic element is identified with its opposite. Within such contexts, one symbol metaphorizes a symbol against which it is usually distinguished.

Symbolic transformations are not mere cultural "play," elaborations upon a range of symbolic idioms. Rather, the impetus for the expression of meaning through transformations derives from the nature of symbolic interrelationships, in conjunction with a social group's intentions in a particular context.

In symbolic transformations, people invert their everyday symbolizations as a response to contexts which demand a certain kind of expression. In societies such as the Mandak, whose cultural traditions create a focal symbol implicitly through differentiations, I suggest that transformations reverse the associations of shared distinctions in order to emphasize the focal symbol in a more direct or inspirational way. Although the contexts of transformations are varied, they all involve the expression of differentiations, not in opposition or as complements, but rather in a manner that implies convertibility between symbols on the basis of their shared similarities as aspects of a focal symbol. In transformational contexts, therefore, distinctions rather than generalizations are still the media of communication, but the former are expressed to emphasize the similarities, the collectivities, of a focal symbol rather than its instrumental parts.

In this chapter I discuss two examples of Mandak transformations, in the eantuing and egirimis complexes. Inversion of symbolic distinctions is not unique to the Mandak but appears in other cultures which emphasize the contrasting and complementary differentiations of a focal symbol. To widen perspective, therefore, after discussing Mandak transformations I will present examples of other Melanesian transformational contexts. The comparisons I selected were chosen on the basis of symbolic patterns analogous to those of the Mandak, in that the cultures appear to display traditions emphasizing differentiating symbols relevant to a focal symbol. The comparable framework is also one in which the sexual dichotomy is central to the culture's social distinctions and transformational contexts. The Melanesian groups I will briefly discuss include the Notsi of central New Ireland, the Karavarans of the Duke of Yorks, and the Iatmul and the Mountain Arapesh, both of the Eastern Sepik District of New Guinea.[1]

Mandak Transformations

eantuing t'bibinet

"the men's house is the clan"

Within the eantuing men create an identification of male with maternal nurture, a female symbol. The men's house serves as a transformational context in which male metaphorizes female nurture. While the eantuing provides a setting for a number of symbolic expressions, I am concerned with it here only as a transformational context.

The sharing or exchanging of food between persons is a very important idiom expressing nurture. When I discussed the eantuing's significance with the Mandak, they inevitably stressed the men's house as an eating place, a source of sustenance. The door to the eantuing should always be open, and hanging inside from a central post should be a basket containing food, such as sweet potato, taro, bananas, and possibly some pork or fish. In contrast, in order to secure the valuables stored within, ekolonu houses are locked when residents are absent. Thus one man explained that when he returns from fishing or some other work in the middle of the day he can always expect to find food in his eantuing. Before

European contact, Mandak men ate all their meals in the men's houses.

The eantuing is also the "source" of important death feasts and other ceremonial occasions in honor of the clan. A death feast must be held in the hamlet of the eantuing where the deceased is buried. Several men stated that the most important work of the ebibinet is in making feasts "come up," and also that the focus of plans for such events is the men's house. For example, in the eankonkomun feast, discussed in chapter 2, the first harvested taro from a new garden is brought to the eantuing of the landowning ewentus. Although both sexes help in the feast's preparations, participation is male-oriented. All speeches at the eankonkomun are made within the eantuing yard, and taro plants from the new garden are distributed among the men in the men's house enclosure rather than among women in the ekolonu. In the three eankonkomun events I attended, although a number of women prepared the cooked feast foods, most returned to their hamlets when the feast began and only a few remained in the ekolonu. The association of men and the eantuing with the female idioms of taro-sharing, and maternal nurture unit suggests a male symbolization of female nurture.

Although from one point of view the eantuing is distinguished from female sharing, since food goes from the ekolonu, where it is prepared by women, to the eantuing, as a transformational context the eantuing itself becomes a nurturing unit—a male image of maternal nurture. It is appropriate that the stone walls which surround the men's house and yard are referred to as *engas ebolowat*, "path of womb rock," and recall female images of womb (*ebolout*) and stone oven (*ebolowat*). The eantuing serves as a context for the expression of a male version of the protective womblike ebibinet unit.

Women are excluded from the eantuing. While there is no female participation in the male metaphorization of maternal nurture, images associated with female are represented by men. In the Mandak's most elaborate traditional death feast, the euli ceremonial complex, women and the powerful euli images and rituals were said to be highly inimical to one another. Elderly men's descriptions of long-past euli ceremonies suggest that the rituals may have served as an elaborate context for the male transformation of female nurture. The carved wooden euli figures, which were said to be inhabited by spirits of deceased clan members, were "fed" by males in the eantuing and were never seen by females. The rituals may have presented the image of men "nurturing" clan ancestors whose spirits were embodied in the carved figures. The euli usually incorporated within one figure both female breasts and a male penis, a combination possibly representing male and female symbolic elements of nurture.

For the transformation of female nurture into a male metaphor, the eantuing excludes women but incorporates certain idioms of the female nurturing symbol. The actual presence of women would confuse the communication of this symbolic inversion, since their participation would call for an opposing male response. At death, however, both sexes are buried in the eantuing yard. As dead substance, the sexual aspect of females which differentiates them from males is negated and they become "social unit." Thus, in the eantuing a maternal nurture unit is represented, a unit which is conceptually "female" and which includes both sexes but is articulated here by males.

The eantuing transformation relies for communication on significations of maternal nurture created in other contexts. The effect of the transformation, I suggest, is to imply the convertibility of male and female elements of nurture, on the basis that both contribute to the social continuity of supportive nurture. In this context, the focal symbol of nurture mediates the similarities of male and female symbolic distinctions. It is the generalized meaning of nurturing continuity that allows for the conversion of opposites into one another. The Mandak cultural tradition emphasizes an indirect mediation of nurture through explicit articulations of its dichotomous forms: male/female, exchanging/sharing, eantuing/ekolonu, and so forth. However, in transformational contexts the generalized concept of nurture is expressed by an inversion of its dichotomies.

The convertibility of certain nurture differentiations into one another is suggested not only in contexts of transformation, but also in certain myths. For example, in the wowera origin myth discussed in chapter 4, a woman is the source of the first wowera, but she gives the ceremonial complex to her male minmin, who performs the first wowera ritual, henceforth an exclusively male ceremonial, at his minmin's death feast. This myth entails a progression of the product of nurture, the wowera, from female to male, a male conversion of female nurture through the wowera ritual.

A Time When All Women Play

The egirimis celebration is another context which provides a setting for the transformation of male/female nurture symbols. Although several symbolic forms are expressed during this occasion, I am concerned here with the egirimis only as a transformational example. Certain female actions during the egirimis communicate a female metaphorization of male nurture. The egirimis, the Mandak say, is "a time when all women play." Although both sexes participate in its preparation and celebration, women are conceptually and functionally its primary participants.

During the usual three-day event, women enact in exaggerated forms certain behavioral features which recall paternal substance symbolizations. In these rituals, women dress as men and perform mock copulations with females of the opposite moiety. Women in cross-moiety relationships "plunder" one another's houses and gardens, taking to demonstrate the indebtedness of an ebibinet for paternal substance nurture. Nimugu plays a primary role in egirimis proceedings: it may be said that her role epitomizes the cross-unit exchanging emphasis of the occasion. At this time any nimugu, but more particularly those who are "blood" to either the paternal or maternal clans of eruwan, publicly expresses paternal substance bonds to a minmin's offspring through food prestations or general joking and buffoonery. The egirimis, it is recalled, marks the birth of a couple's first child, the eruwan, symbolically the beginning of cross-unit nurture between two subclans. It is an occasion when the two social units "eat one another's food."

While men attend the egirimis and eat together in the sponsoring hamlet's eantuing, they do not assume active roles in expressing cross-unit relationships. In the two egirimises I attended, the men turned their backs on the women's antics in the ekolonu, for the women were said to "have no shame" at this time.

As a transformational context, the egirimis associates "female" with "male" nurture—the cross-unit exchange of nurture. The metaphorization of male nurture by female is achieved by women "playing" male roles suggestive of cross-unit symbolizations—the prestation of procreative substance and exchanges of food, wealth, and so forth. The transformation implies the convertibility between male and female symbolic elements on the basis of their similar functions as nurturing actions. Through the focal symbol of nurture, the Mandak mediate their transformation of male/female symbolizations. In the egirimis, in which eruwan serves as a symbolic idiom of procreative nurture, the Mandak focus not on contrasting male and female, but on expressing their generalized similarities as complementary aspects of nurture.

Melanesian Comparisons

The Notsi

In the preceding chapter, I suggested that although the Notsi and the Mandak share a similar symbolic orientation in social distinctions, they contrast in their relative focus on the articulation of sharing and exchanging. The hypothesized Notsi emphasis on exchanging as a continuing nurturing relationship which integrates sharing units is reiterated in certain transformational contexts.

At feasts celebrating birth, marriage, and male circumcision, Notsi women make stylized speeches about their husband's daily food contributions.[2] For example, in rituals accompanying male circumcision, the wives of the circumcised boys' *tatas* (MB, etc.) stand around food being presented to their hubands' *tsringis* (ZS, etc.) while, one at a time, each woman speaks of her spouse's food-providing abilities.[3] Each speaker typically carries an implement associated with male labor—a fishing net, knife, hatchet, basket, or spear—with which she gesticulates as she delivers her address in a humorous style.

Such ritual speeches by women serve as transformational contexts for the female metaphorization of male cross-unit exchanging. The speeches, conjoining male cross-unit nurturing with female suggest a convertibility between male and female nurture symbolizations on the basis of similar functions in the support of social continuity. In these contexts, as in the Mandak examples just discussed, the Notsi mediate their focal symbol of nurture by inverting its differentiating symbols. By conjoining aspects of the sexual dichotomy within a single form, the nurturing similarities of male and female are given more explicit expression than in the everyday differentiating forms. Thus the focal symbol of nurture as social support and continuity is communicated by bringing together a female image (speakers) with a male representation—in references to the husbands' cross-unit provision of food.

Other Notsi transformations in which female metaphorizes male cross-unit exchanging are suggested by contexts entailing mock fights and play between women of opposite moieties. Such ritual behavior is evoked by the announcement of a pregnancy.[4] Although Powdermaker's descriptions of the female "play fights" are confusing, it appears that women of the moiety opposite that of a pregnant woman "attack" and receive food exchanges from women of her own moiety. After a birth, women of opposite moieties also fight one another, although on this occasion it appears that either moiety may initiate the battles.[5] These contexts, I suggest, associate female nurture, expressed by the women, and male nurture, the latter represented in the emphasis on the cross-unit exchange of nurture.

There are obvious similarities between the Notsi female ritual responses to a pregnancy or birth and the Mandak egirimis celebration. The Mandak say that many aspects of their present egirimis have been borrowed from the Notsi, particularly the emphasis on female "play." Former Mandak egirimis celebrations were simpler and included nimugu joking, distributions of coconuts and taro, and fewer occurrences of female play. I suggest that the Notsi have elaborated contexts entailing female metaphorization of male cross-unit nurture. In addition to mock battles between women, there are numerous occasions when women of opposite moieties exchange taro reciprocally—at birth feasts, in a feast celebrating a girl's first menses, and at a marriage.[6] The Mandak "eat of one another's food," at the egirimis feast, but otherwise taro and other foods are given in a single direction at this time by nimugus to their minmin's children. In contrast, the Notsi tamangaina (FZ) engages in a reciprocal exchange of taro with her matonga's (B) children.[7] In summary, in ritual contexts the Notsi have emphasized cross-unit exchanges between women and the metaphorization by females of male cross-unit exchanging. This Notsi contrast with the Mandak procedure reiterates the hypothesized difference between the two groups in their focus on the articulation of sharing/exchanging. The Mandak enact fewer contexts of female metaphorization of male nurture than the Notsi, but the Mandak contexts occur almost entirely in conjunction with expressions of procreative relationships, whereas the Notsi contexts focus on both procreative and affinal relationships. Thus the Notsi emphasize exchanging as an integrative element between social units both in their everyday symbolic forms and in their transformational contexts.

The Notsi malanggan complex suggests another transformational context. Malanggan rituals occur in association with mortuary rites and male circumcision, and they involve the transfer of the right to own and construct a particular malanggan carving.[8] A malanggan is purchased by one or more men in honor of a deceased person or a male initiate. In Lewis's examples of malanggan exchanges, he cites more cases of patronages in cross-unit than same-unit relationships.[9] An example of a "cross-unit patronage" is when a man, X, with the help of his own clan or subclan, buys the rights to a particular malanggan which he will have constructed in honor of a deceased person in his wife's clan. The subsequent "ownership" of this malanggan is with his wife's clan. I suggest that the Notsi malanggan contexts involve a male metaphorization of female nurture in much the same way as Mandak males metaphorize maternal nurture through their feasting ceremonies. Females are excluded from participating in the malanggan complex, although they may take part as clan members in the exchanges and are important adjuncts in preparing and executing accompanying feasts. By creating and sustaining the malanggan rituals, the Notsi men present a ceremonial version of female nurture. Since malanggans involve patronages for cross-unit relationships as frequently as same-unit patronages, if not more so, the Notsi display another context for emphasis on exchanging. The cross-unit malanggan patronages described by Lewis occur in both procreative and affinal relationships.[10]

Karavar

The tubuan ceremonial complex of the Karavar people of the Duke of Yorks presents another transformational context involving male and female symbolic elements.[11] In Karavaran culture, the sexual dichotomy figures significantly in distinctions of interpersonal and inter-group relationships. Female is associated with social unit membership—matrilineal clans and moieties—productivity, and social continuity.[12] Male is conjoined with social order, the control of inherently disordered human nature.[13]

The tubuan cult includes the following features. It is an exclusively male ritual complex: women are forbidden to come near the men's ritual area during tubuan activities, they are excluded from tubuan construction secrets, and they must avoid tubuan figures when the latter enter the village.[14] Women cannot conduct their exclusively female rituals when tubuan activities are in process.[15] A tubuan figure is "female," represents a particular matrilineal clan, is called by the name of a clan's ancestress or some other female clan name, and is described through various maternal images.[16] The tubuan figure becomes highly charged with a dangerous spirit during the final stages of its construction by a male ritual adept.[17] The completion of the tubuan figures initiates a period called the "tubuan peace" when people should "act properly" and are fined by a special *kilung* court for certain kinds of antisocial actions. This court does not deal with the usual secular offenses such as divorce, which are dealt with by the *vurkurai* court during nonritual times.[18]

According to Errington's study, male is symbolically associated with the taming of innate human disorder, through the exchange of shell valuables within the context of moiety.[19] Disorder, while characteristic of human social interaction in general, also is particularly associated with female.[20] If females ensure one kind of social continuity through procreative productivity, men complement them in the interests of social continuity through their efforts to curb disorder.

The tubuan complex suggests a convertibility of male and female symbolic elements on the basis of their similarities as co-contributors to ordered social continuity. The male participants in the tubuan complex enact a ceremonial version of female productivity in creating and sustaining the "female" tubuan figures. Yet these figures are imbued with a "highly dangerous" spirit, which is controlled only by male ritual adepts. The tubuan context thus is a male expression of female productivity which is both a distinction of social continuity and also an image of disorder which must be tamed.

The Karavaran expression of convertibility between male and female symbolic distinctions is also glimpsed in the tubuan origin myth.[21] According to this myth, the secrets of tubuan construction and rituals were given to a woman, who then made the first tubuan figure. However, her husband forcibly took it from her, and ever since the tubuan has been an exclusively male ritual. The tubuan origin myth suggests a progression from female origin of the tubuan (matrilineal continuity) to male ceremonial productivity. As in the eantuing complex, however, while females are excluded from the tubuan rituals as actual participants, they are incorporated as members of social units represented by the tubuan figures.[22]

The Iatmul

Another example of a transformation of male/female symbolic elements is suggested by the *naven* complex of the Iatmul in the Eastern Sepik District of New Guinea.[23] These rituals center around stylized forms of interaction between a man as *wau* (MB, etc.) and his *laua* (ZS, ZD, etc.).[24] In response to recognized "cultural" achievements of his laua, wau's reactions include dressing in widow's weeds; being called "*nyame*" (mother) by laua; performing exaggerated gestures with female connotations, such as rubbing the cleft of his buttocks along male laua's leg, actions suggesting "giving birth" to female laua, and mock copulation with his wife, dressed as a male; and presenting food to laua, who reciprocates with shell valuables. The occasions for naven rituals are when laua performs certain actions for the first time, such as killing certain animals, using a stone ax, killing a man, and planting particular crops. When laua performs actions seen as characteristic of the laua/wau relationship—playing the sacred flutes of wau's clan, for example—when laua boasts in his wau's presence, and when there is a recognized change in laua's social status, wau responds with naven behavior.[25]

While the naven rituals are complex and may be considered from numerous viewpoints, I suggest that at one level of expression naven is a symbolic transformation analogous to the examples considered for the Mandak, Notsi, and Karavarans. Naven is a context in which male metaphorizes female symbolic elements. A pattern which may be used to describe Iatmul symbolic distinctions equates "female" with achievement, productivity, blood, cross-unit relationships, and exchanging, in complementary opposition to "male," identified with same-unit relationships, sharing, and physical substance (bone). The Iatmul view the person's "cultural" abilities as the achievement of his maternal clan, while the person shares one kind of physical substance (bone), food, wealth, work, and so forth, with his paternal social unit.[26]

In the naven rituals, a transformation is suggested by wau's "female" behavior and his identification with laua's maternal clan. Yet a male element is also represented by wau's "maleness," for his transvestism is an obvious masquerading, as indicated by the exaggerated, mocking gestures with which he performs naven rituals.[27] Wau is a male in a symbolically "male" clan; yet in naven rituals he represents his social unit as "female" in cross-unit interactions with his laua. Naven rituals imply a convertibility between male social-unit solidarity and female "cultural" productivity. A focal symbol of Iatmul social relationships may be represented as "social continuity." Since it would necessitate considerable discussion to contrast the Iatmul "social continuity" with that defined for the Mandak, I use the terms only as a general gloss to refer to the focal symbol of Iatmul social distinctions, one which incorporates the sexual dichotomy and other major symbolic social distinctions. In the naven rituals, the focal symbol mediates the transformation of male/female symbolic elements, to communicate a conversion of female achievement into male group solidarity, or a male version of female achievement *for* the social unit.

In many ways the naven rituals recall the nimugu social category of the Mandak. Nimugu as FZ communicates cross-unit symbolizations through mock plunder and joking behavior toward her minmin's children. Nimugu expresses paternal substance by emphasizing the exchanging aspects of her minmin's children's relationship to her clan. Among the Iatmul, wau, as male, plays a more obvious opposite sex role in the naven rituals. Both nimugu and wau personify their social unit's contribution to another clan's growth and continuity. Through such actions, nimugu/nimugu and wau/laua relationships become contexts for symbolic transformations. For the Mandak, nimugu conjoins female with an expression of male cross-unit nurture: for the Iatmul, wau associates male with female cross-unit achievement. These symbolic inversions are mediated through focal symbols which communicate generalized social continuity and the convertibility of male and female symbolizations as co-contributors to social continuity.

While the Iatmul person is a member of his father's social unit, he is also, Bateson suggests, associated with his mother's clan.[28] Thus a man may blow the sacred flutes of his wau's clan and in other ways honor his wau's clan totems. A person receives two sets of personal names, one from his own social unit and another from his maternal clan. A male laua is expected to help his wau in formal debates in the ceremonial house and to speak for his maternal clan.[29] Laua exchanges with wau when the latter gives him maternal clan secrets and spells.[30] Mortuary rites are performed in part by the deceased's paternal clan, in part by the maternal clan.[31] A person's spirit after death appears to have a double existence, one under the personal names given by wau and another through a "rebirth" in his son's son.[32] In summary, while the Iatmul person is a member of his paternal clan, he also is involved in a recognized supportive relationship with his maternal clan.

Naven rituals involve a response by wau to his laua's demonstrations of cultural abilities (a recognition of maternal achievement), or laua's expressions of relationships with wau's social unit, as for example when laua blows the sacred flutes of wau's clan.[33] Bateson analyzes the naven rituals in part through two identifications of the wau/laua relationship: one in which wau is associated with his sister, laua's mother, and the other in which laua is identified with his own F, so that the wau/laua relationship is constituted as one between brothers-in-law.[34] I suggest that while these identifications are reflected in the naven interactions, the behavior of wau/laua also is

Karavaran tubuan, which *is* a symbolic expression of female social continuity, and laua's first achievements, which *are* symbolic forms of female productivity. The Mandak eantuing, the Karavaran tubuan, and the Iatmul laua's achievements are forms of female symbolizations which are created in other contexts. There is no need to express ritual "embodiment" of maternal nurture through *female* participants. To do so would add nothing to the communication of maternal nurture, for it would be a redundant symbolic form. By considering both contextual occasions, status change and a potentially redundant symbolic form, I suggest that contexts of symbolic transformation occur in situations which call for an expression of both sides of a symbolic dialogue. These occasions obviously are concerned with one side of a dichotomy (eantuing, tubuan, naven) or concern a status change predominantly involving one side of a dichotomy (egirimis, Notsi female transformations, initiation rites). In both situations, there is a need to communicate, more directly than through everyday differentiation, the junction of distinctions within the similarities of the focal symbol. For example, the maternal nurture symbolization of the Mandak social unit is expressed in many different forms as female, sharing, same-unit, nurture. In a context in which the maternal nurture unit is ritually incorporated (a place, burials, a source of feasts, etc.), the Mandak have expressed the female social unit through its opposite—male— thereby reconstituting maternal nurture within both differentiations to emphasize social unit as nurturing continuity. Thus in the naven rituals, an individual's growing into clan membership (first achievements) is met by the Iatmul with an inverted male/female form which communicates a continuity encompassing both male/ female distinctions. The tubuan figures, which *are* a female symbolization, are expressed through male to reconstitute female social continuity and male order as complements of a generalized social order. In the comparative cultures, none of the differentiating symbols can stand by itself, since all exist within one or more dichotomies as complementary parts of an implicit focal symbol. In most contexts, these distinctions are extended in meaning by further metaphorization with other concepts and a continual dialogue with opposing or complementary distinctions or both. However, in contexts which are the symbolic forms, as created in other contexts, or which mark a significant change of relationships, the generalized focal symbol of sociality is expressed by inverting elements of its own distinctive symbolic forms.

8   Conclusion

Cultural meaning is created and extended through shared symbolizations. Extension results from continual reinterpretation of symbols through incorporation or contrast with other concepts. Communication of meaning is easier when particular symbolic elements occur in many contexts. Since each contextual symbolic form both distinguishes and is defined by other relevant symbolic expressions, the meaning of cultural metaphors is often complex and capable of infinite elaboration. The shared understandings of a social group emerge from the reiteration and innovation of cultural concepts in numerous interrelated contexts.

The value of a symbolic focus in cultural analysis lies in its emphasis on crucial, though often ignored, features of cultural meaning and cross-cultural interpretation. The concept of cultural symbolizations deals with the relational aspects of cultural creativity—the development of meaning through contextual associations of variant expressions. An awareness of the process whereby cultural content is the product of conceptual relationships should remind us that inquiry never ends in the comfortable seat of our own cultural understanding. For example, to bracket the Mandak expression "woman is the clan" with my own cultural conceptualization of "woman" and "clan" circumvents an effort to understand this Mandak symbolic idiom. Of course, all cross-cultural analyses involve premature termination of inquiry, but the conclusion must carry with it a sense of the other culture's symbolizations.

In this final chapter I will summarize, review, and reconsider the interpretive pattern of symbols in general terms. I will bring together my ideas about the relationship of the Mandak to the nurture symbols in terms of their emphasis on and articulations of their cultural concepts. Attention will therefore be directed to general modes of symbolic interrelationship—opposition, complementarity, and integration. I will also consider here the varying kinds of commitment the Mandak appear to make to their nurture symbols.

A pattern of Mandak symbolizations has been discussed through interrelationships of a focal symbol, nurture, and three differentiating symbols, maternal nurture, paternal substance, and affinal nurture. I have suggested that through these symbols the Mandak create a significant part of their social world. The Mandak person is initiated and supported through interpersonal and intergroup nurturing relationships. While the focal symbol of nurture constitutes the positive aspects of the social environment, nurture as a set of sustaining social relationships coexists with negative human intentions and actions. The inimical side of human interactions is particularly apparent today in Mandak observations about the prevalence of sorcery in their society. I found no indication, however, that the Mandak believe their social life to be fundamentally disordered, as Errington suggests for the Karavarans of the Duke of Yorks.[1] Social groups are constituted positively through the articulated variants of nurturing relationships. The negative side of sociality is man's ability to harm others. These observations about man coexist in a tenuous balance. Mandak social continuity depends not so much on the negation of individual destructive propensities as on the deliberate, slow, and orderly establishment of nurturing relationships *in spite of* harmful individual tendencies. Because the Mandak do not often directly articulate their focal symbol of nurture, there are few spoken moralities about the positive force of nurture. Thus nurture and its antithesis present the boundaries of a social world: nurture does not eradicate individual antisocial motivations, but it opposes them in intentions and results.

Individuals make choices about the boundaries of their supportive relationships. The Mandak person maintains a continuous dialogue with his world—a dialectic of inclusion and exclusion of nurturing interactions. For most purposes the individual separates himself from various nonhuman socialities—the worlds of the embau and erogas. These nonhuman domains are perceived as reflections of the human world, but generally the Mandak maintain a clear distinction and separation between themselves and these other domains. Through opposition, they define a human mode of existence, as in differences of cooked versus raw foods and bush and sea versus human settlement. Occasionally the domains connect, as when an eu gives a ceremonial song-dance form to a sleeping person or when an egas harms someone. Thus nonhuman socialities serve as a source both of danger to humans and of creativity.

Within the world of human relationships, the Mandak person engages in another dialectic of inclusion/exclusion of nurturing interactions. The moral force of nurturing relationships is expanded and contracted to form, maintain, and change the social boundaries of political factions, hamlets, villages, and language groups. In diverse contexts and for different individuals, the supportive quality of group intrarelationships varies greatly. For example, at a feast in another language group, people from Pinikindu often appear as a unit (separated by sex), with both Emalam and Erangam males sharing a temporary men's house in the host village. Returning to their own hamlets, however, these people immediately constrict and differentiate their nurturing boundaries. A Big Man extends his network of power through maternal nurture, paternal substance, and affinal nurture relationships to enlarge and focus his sharing/exchanging interactions to the best advantage for the exercise of his influence. Nurture, while descriptive and constituted of generalized supportive social relationships, may be articulated by quite dissimilarly composed groups according to different contexts and individual interests.

The focal symbol of nurture is not usually articulated as a social ideal in contrast to individual antisocial motives and actions; rather, it is expressed through elaborations of its distinctive features as maternal nurture, paternal substance, and affinal nurture. Nurture thus has many faces, many voices, but no intrinsic form of its own except as an abstraction of the articulated "faces" and "voices." In a sense, nurture is "counterinvented" through the differentiation of its parts, a mode that Wagner suggests is common for tribal, peasant, and certain other cultural traditions.[2] Nurture *is* the background of similarities against which male/female, exchanging/sharing are being expressed.

"To procreate" (-vasik) expresses the focal symbol, nurture; yet procreation is generally articulated only in relation to *either* male or female progenitors. In defining their social categories, therefore, the Mandak never conjoined male and female as subjects of -vasik, although the person's social framework receives its outline from the dual nature of procreative efforts. Procreation is expressed through only one of its differentiated forms, male or female. Thus both nanga and tamak nurture emandak and enek, not by merging but by complementing their roles. Male and female present contrasting manifestations of procreation: the former gives substance, the latter provides sustenance. However, these distinctive functions are at the same time unitary as supportive nurture. Through their differentiating roles, tamak and nanga create implicitly the undifferentiated synthesis of nurture.

Underlying the distinctions made by symbolic articulations is the Mandak concept of dichotomy—that society is fundamentally constituted in two parts—and that all individuals are "like" certain people and "different from" others in a bipartite social world. Emalam and Erangam are the Mandak social objectifications of this basic human dichotomy. Moiety membership is explained as the social recognition of the fact that people are born one of two possible physical types. The outward forms of this division are minor nonfunctional attributes, such as different styles of walking and contrasting patterns of lines on the hands. All peoples display this duality, although not all societies recognize and use the differences for social purposes. The Mandak have realized this inherent social dichotomy in their moiety division. While they also say that a person receives his moiety name from his nanga, moiety membership is not explained in the same nurturing terms as for the ebibinet and ewentus. There is no recognized way for an individual to change moieties: a person *is* Emalam or Erangam from birth, or, for an outsider, becomes so by marriage into the society. In the latter case, the individual belongs to the moiety opposite that of his/her spouse. Sharing can never extend across moiety boundaries, nor can exchanging create exclusive sharing units within a dual division. The moiety birds, Emalam and Erangam, do not reflect a recognized species dichotomy in any functional or complementary sense. The Mandak feel they have recognized a basic split in human types and constituted a natural dichotomy along complementary lines to create their social world of nurture.

Ebibinets are not conceived as subdivisions within Emalam or Erangam; rather, each clan was once simply allocated to one of the dual divisions. There are recognized means for an individual to change ebibinet membership within the same moiety—through erembeke for a woman, through exchanging actions for a man. A person may extend sharing relationships widely within his moiety through the ewentamat relationship. Individuals thus deliberately articulate particular maternal nurture relationships within the moiety and certain paternal substance and affinal nurture relationships across moiety boundaries. People create and emphasize their own networks of cooperation by different patterns of exchanging/sharing between and within moieties. However, the moiety division remains unalterable and constitutes a fixed structure whereby "being like" is symbolically "sharing" and "being different" is symbolically exchanging. While Emalam and Erangam identifications for the individual may not be created through symbolic expression, moiety organization serves the widest range for the articulation of sameness/difference of personal identity as differentiations of nurture. Persons share within the moiety as expressions of their "sameness" and exchange across moiety boundaries as forms of "difference." Sharing is symbolically extended through the concept of "female" and becomes a reciprocal interaction which *is* female and being-of-one-kind. Exchanging is metaphorically "male" and becomes a reciprocal interaction which *is* male and being-of-unlike-kind. The nurturing structure of relationships has thus been integrated around and within the recognition of a basic human dichotomy.

Nurturing relationships complementarize the basic dualistic nature of society. While male/female and exchanging/sharing become actions and identities manifesting a bipartite world, the sexual and reciprocal dichotomies are integrated as complementary aspects of nurture. Although male and female are expressed as oppositions to one another in response to an inherent differentiation, male and female are also articulated as complementary forms of nurture. In forms of mutual exclusion and contrast, the sexual dichotomy is expressed through differentiation of male/female in spatial arrangements, activity spheres, interests, rituals, social roles, and so forth. At the same time, sexual separation is structured by the complementary relationship of nurturing functions. Both sexual symbolizations are necessary for the initiation and continuation of nurture—for social survival and continuity. The Mandak individual and the particular social units of ebibinet and ewentus exist through interaction of male and female concepts. "Male" initiates and exchanges nurture: "female" continues and shares nurture.

Reciprocal interactions also reflect a basic dichotomy in the separation and contrast of exchanging and sharing. These two interactions are differentiations of a single mode of behavior—the expression of relationship through prestations of things external to either party. If reciprocal interaction is an expressive social form among people of "like" and "unlike" categories, it follows that the relationships communicated through reciprocal actions will also reflect this duality. By giving and receiving "things," the Mandak person states his similarity or dissimilarity to others. This expression is structured by differences inherent in the moiety division, while articulations are creative within and between particular clans and subclans.

An outsider's view of Mandak symbolic distinctions and the Mandak's commitment to their own cultural concepts may involve contrasting interpretations of the nurture pattern. From the outsider's viewpoint, the Mandak appear to be directing their cultural energies upon differentiations in terms of opposition and contrast. I suggest, however, that the Mandak do not see their own symbolic pattern in terms of maintaining distinctions (between male/female, exchanging/sharing). For the Mandak, relationships are founded on an inherent dichotomy which is not being elaborated so much as being "used" to create and continue a social purpose and continuity. The difference between these two viewpoints is important in regard to the total signification of the symbol pattern, for such meaning incorporates not only symbolic content but also the way people relate to their own symbolizations. This "commitment" is part of the cultural pattern but is not contained within the symbolizations themselves. The same symbols, nurture, maternal nurture, paternal substance, and affinal nurture, might be expressed through a different kind of commitment to produce a quite different signification in the total symbol pattern. Symbolizations are not mere guides to action, for involved with their expression is a people's sense of purpose or futility—of the malleable or immutable nature of the world.

The Mandak cultural tradition encourages further symbolization through dichotomous contrasts and complementary actions rather than efforts to integrate through negation of differences. "Integration," in both a cultural and social sense, is for the Mandak a product of differentiation rather than the negation or slurring of distinctions. Thus, in contexts of symbolic transformation when the Mandak intention is to express the "similarities" of nurture, their integrative effort is accomplished by articulating the differences in an inverted fashion to suggest convertibility between differences on the basis of similarities. Integration, as an effort against cultural disjunction or social fission, is accomplished by using or realizing differences, distinctions believed to be inherent, rather than through obliterating them.

The nurture symbols constitute a special kind of cultural language which is communicated, recreated, and modified daily in the social interactions of Mandak individuals and groups. These interpretive symbols have been presented and discussed in terms of the various features which together contribute to their total meaning. Yet these significations lose their own complexity when juxtaposed with the imaginative and often perplexing intricacies of ongoing social lives in central New Ireland. I hope that this interpretation will yield an understanding of the creative and compelling cultural perceptions of the Mandak people.

Notes

Introduction

1. Roy Wagner, *Habu*.
2. Ibid., p. 5.
3. David M. Schneider, "What Is Kinship All About?" pp. 51-60.

Chapter 1

1. David Lithgow and Orev Claasen, *Languages of the New Ireland District*, p. 3.
2. Ibid.
3. Ibid., pp. 5-6.
4. R. Berle Clay, "Archaeological Reconnaissance in Central New Ireland," pp. 1-17.
5. E. W. Pearson Chinnery, *Studies of the Native Population of the East Coast of New Ireland*, p. 32.
6. R. F. R. Scragg, *Depopulation in New Ireland; A Study of Demography and Fertility*; idem, "Population Change over Twenty Years in Four Rural New Guinea Communities."
7. Of the present marriages in Pinikindu Village (a total of 67): 38 marriages were made within the village, 21 marriages involved one spouse born outside the village, 8 marriages involved a spouse born outside but of a Pinikindu-born parent, and 20 persons (8 males, 12 females) have married and moved out of the village. In regard to the latter group of 20, 7 have moved off New Ireland, 6 to other language areas within New Ireland, and 7 to other Mandak villages. Of the 29 outsiders living in Pinikindu, 22 come from other Mandak villages (14 from Northern Mandak villages), 3 from other New Ireland language groups, and 4 from other areas of Papua New Guinea (New Britain, New Guinea, Tabar, and Lihir).
8. Douglas Oliver, *A Solomon Island Society: Kinship and Leadership among the Siuai of Bougainville*, 2d ed. (Boston: Beacon Press, 1967), p. 15.
9. R. Berle Clay, "The Persistence of Traditional Settlement Pattern: An Example from Central New Ireland," p. 53.

Chapter 2

1. David M. Schneider, *American Kinship*, pp. 23-25.
2. Frederick Errington, "Indigenous Ideas of Order, Time, and Transition in a New Guinea Cargo Movement," pp. 255-68.

Chapter 3

1. A. R. Radcliffe-Brown, *Structure and Function in Primitive Society*, pp. 67, 70.
2. Harold W. Scheffler and Floyd G. Lounsbury, *A Study in Structural Semantics: The Siriono Kinship System* (Englewood Cliffs, N.J.: Prentice-Hall, 1971), pp. 51–52.
3. David M. Schneider, "What Is Kinship All About? pp. 51–60.

Chapter 4

1. Phillip H. Lewis, *The Social Context of Art in Northern New Ireland*, p. 106; Augustin Kramer, *Die Malanngane von Tombara* (Munich: Georg Müller, 1925), pp. 67–70.
2. A similar wowera origin myth was recorded by Kramer, and a different version was found among the Notsi: Lewis, *The Social Context of Art*, pp. 103–7; Kramer, *Die Malanngane*, pp. 67–68.
3. An example of some of the complexities of the Melanesian "shame" concept may be seen in Andrew Strathern, "Why Is Shame on the Skin?" *Ethnology* 14, no. 4 (1975):347–56.
4. In the euli ceremonies, men for whom the right was purchased received a name associated with a carved euli figure. *Labakarat* was the name of one euli, and it was the only one which might be used to effect a female minmin's suicide.
5. The Mandak suggested that this expected response by a man to gossip about his minmin's adultery acted as a deterrent to adultery in the past. Others said that it served only as a sanction against indiscreet adulteries. All persons with whom I spoke concurred that adultery is a social problem today and a common occurrence.
6. The Mandak say that men and women have different kinds of "talk." Sexual linguistic contrasts seem to involve the exclusive use of synonyms by males or females, but I found only a few actual examples of this. For example, men and women use different words to refer to a newborn male child.

Chapter 5

1. In 1970–71, out of a total of 67 marriages in Pinikindu Village, only 7 marriages involved one spouse marrying into his/her father's ebibinet.
2. The Konos women's speeches were very much like the stylized Notsi female speeches to be discussed in chapter 7. The Konos affinal ewentus may have been active in this egirimis because of the lack of blood connections for eruwan and eruwan's MM—eruwan's father was a man from New Guinea and eruwan's MM was married to a man who lacked clan representation in the Pinikindu area.
3. While in most cases the actual social unit involved in exchanges is the subclan, the Mandak often refer to such interactions as between ebibinets rather than ewentuses. The group of individuals encompassed by these references is clearly understood, but the unit designation may be generalized as "ebibinet."

Chapter 6

1. Hortense Powdermaker, "Report on Fieldwork in New Ireland," p. 357; idem, "Mortuary Rites in New Ireland," pp. 26–43; idem, "Vital Statistics in New

Ireland," pp. 351–75; idem, "Feasts in New Ireland: The Social Functions of Eating," pp. 236–47; idem, *Life in Lesu*; idem, *Stranger and Friend*, pp. 49–125.

2. Phillip H. Lewis, *The Social Context of Art in Northern New Ireland*; idem, "Changing Memorial Ceremonial in Northern New Ireland," pp. 141–53.

3. Lewis, *The Social Context of Art*, pp. 25–44; Powdermaker, "Mortuary Rites in New Ireland"; "Feasts in New Ireland"; idem, *Life in Lesu*, pp. 33–39, 43–80, 308–19.

4. Powdermaker, *Life in Lesu*, pp. 45–57.

5. Ibid., pp. 43–44, 326.

6. Ibid., pp. 159–60.

7. Ibid., p. 147.

8. Lewis, *The Social Context of Art*, pp. 58, 61, 63, 86, 96–98, 110–11, 116, 131.

9. Powdermaker, *Life in Lesu*, p. 78.

10. Ibid., p. 98.

11. Ibid., p. 147.

12. Ibid., p. 91.

13. Ibid., p. 327.

14. Ibid., p. 52.

15. Ibid., p. 244.

16. Ibid., pp. 53–54.

17. Ibid., p. 75.

18. Ibid., p. 119.

19. Gregory Bateson, *Naven*, pp. 289–91.

Chapter 7

1. Notsi: Phillip H. Lewis, *The Social Context of Art in Northern New Ireland*; idem, "Changing Memorial Ceremonial in Northern New Ireland," pp. 141–53; Hortense Powdermaker, "Report on Fieldwork in New Ireland," p. 357; idem, "Mortuary Rites in New Ireland," pp. 26–43; idem, "Vital Statistics in New Ireland," pp. 351–75; idem, "Feasts in New Ireland: The Social Functions of Eating," pp. 236–47; idem, *Life in Lesu*; idem, *Stranger and Friend*; Karavarans: Frederick Errington, "Indigenous Ideas of Order, Time and Transition in a New Guinea Cargo Movement," pp. 255–68; idem, *Karavar*; Iatmul: Gregory Bateson, *Naven*; Mountain Arapesh: Margaret Mead, *The Mountain Arapesh*, vols. 1, 2, 3.

2. Powdermaker, *Life in Lesu*, pp. 73–74, 110–12, 137, 148–49; idem, *Stranger and Friend*, p. 109.

3. Powdermaker, *Life in Lesu*, p. 110.

4. Ibid., pp. 60–62.

5. Ibid., pp. 65–66.

6. Ibid., pp. 75, 142, 144–45, 151.

7. Ibid., p. 75.

8. Lewis, *The Social Context of Art*, p. 45.

9. Ibid., pp. 58, 61, 82–83, 86–87, 96–97, 111–13, 116, 130–32, 162; idem, "Changing Memorial," pp. 147–48.

10. A mask or malanggan can be purchased to honor both affinal and procreative bonds of the patron; Lewis, *The Social Context of Art*, p. 116. In buying rights to have a mask carved, a man honors his wife's deceased parents and at the same time his son, an initiate in a malanggan complex involving mortuary and initiation rites.

11. Errington, *Karavar*.
12. Ibid., pp. 58, 63, 120-21, 200-201.
13. Ibid., pp. 58-65.
14. Ibid., pp. 88, 202-5.
15. Ibid., pp. 206-7.
16. Ibid., pp. 118, 202.
17. Ibid., p. 166.
18. Ibid., pp. 166-75.
19. Ibid., pp. 35, 59-60.
20. Ibid., pp. 58-65, 120-21, 201-02.
21. Ibid., p. 114.
22. Ibid., pp. 114-15, 118-21.
23. Bateson, *Naven*.
24. Ibid., pp. 95-96. Naven rituals were said to be performed more by classificatory wau/laua than by "true" wau/laua.
25. Ibid., pp. 6-22.
26. Ibid., pp. 37-38, 42, 74-78.
27. Ibid., pp. 12-13, 78, 84-85, 202.
28. Ibid., p. 42.
29. Ibid., pp. 8, 37, 42.
30. Ibid., p. 37.
31. Ibid., pp. 47-48.
32. Ibid., p. 42.
33. Ibid., p. 8.
34. Ibid., pp. 74-75.
35. Ibid., p. 74.
36. Ibid.
37. Ibid., pp. 43-44.
38. Ibid., p. 40.
39. Ibid., pp. 14-17, 214.
40. Ibid., pp. 81-82: in interpreting two responses of wau in naven, presenting his buttocks to laua and wau's exclamation, *"Lan men to!"* Bateson's alternative interpretations cannot be ruled out—the former as giving birth, the latter as a general expression of submissiveness.
41. Mead, *Mountain Arapesh*, vols. 1, 2, 3.
42. Ibid., 3:49-67.
43. Ibid., 3:49-51.
44. Ibid., 3:49-50; 2:257-58, 290-91.
45. Ibid., 2:257-58.
46. Ibid., 2:290-91.
47. Ibid., 2:42-43, 432-38; 3:50-51.
48. Nancy D. Munn, *Walbiri Iconography*, pp. 171-73, 188, 194, 211-21.
49. Roy Wagner, *The Invention of Culture*, p. 119.
50. Ibid., pp. 58-59, 119.

CHAPTER 8

1. Frederick Errington, *Karavar*, pp. 19-20.
2. Roy Wagner, *The Invention of Culture*, p. 51.

Glossary of Mandak Terms

This glossary briefly defines Northern Mandak words which appear more than once in the text. The terms follow the particular dialect used in Pinikindu Village. All Northern Mandak nouns have an obligatory prefix *e-*. This prefix has been disregarded in alphabetizing the glossary. Kinship terms are not included.

aulit: au′-lit
> To start again, to begin again

eanis: e-a-nis′
> A traditional Mandak dance in which a particular kind of mask is used, known in Neo-Melanesian as Tatanua

eankonkomun: e-an-kɔn′-kɔ-mun
> A feast which marks the first harvest from a new taro garden

eantuing: e-an-tu-iŋ′
> The men's house and its enclosed yard and burial grounds

ebibinet: e-bɨ′-bɨ-net
> Matrilineal, exogamous clan

ebolout: e-bol′-o-ut
> Womb

ebolowat: e-bol′-o-wat
> A pile of heated stones used for baking food

egas (plural: erogas): e-gas′ (e′-ɨo-gas)
> Nonhuman beings: every living person has an egas double

egirimis: e-gɨɨ′-ɨ-mis
> A feast which honors a couple's firstborn child

egiskebot: e-gis′-ke-bɔt
> A ritual which expresses the end of blood relationships between ego (as firstborn child, and his/her

sibling group) and the subclans of his/her MMF, MFF, FFF, and FMF.

egursay: e-gur̃'-say

> To pay for a pig at a feast

ekarambis: e-kar̃'-am-bis

> The second of a series of feasts following a death

ekolonu: e-kol'-o-nu

> An area of a hamlet which includes the family dwelling houses and cooking area

elam: e-lam'

> A type of men's dance which has been told to a man while he is sleeping by the spirits of the dead, the embau

eleplep: e-lep'-lep

> A type of woman's dance told to a sleeping person by the spirits of the dead, the embau

emagai: e-ma^n-gai'

> Shame

Emalam: E-ma-lam'

> One of the Northern Mandak moieties and the name of a variety of sea eagle (*Haliaetus leucogaster*)

emandak: e-man-dak'

> Man, boy

embinow: e^m'-bi-now

> To mark someone at a feast to contribute a pig for a subsequent feast

momoton: mɔ'-mɔ-tɔn

> True

enat: e-nat'

> Blood

enda: e^n-da'

> Blood

engas ebolowat: eŋ-as' e-bol'-o-wat

> Dry stone wall, particularly that which surrounds a men's house

-puke: -pu-kay'

> To marry

Erangam: E-r̃an-gam'

> One of the Northern Mandak moieties and the name of a variety of sea hawk (*Pandion leucocephalus*)

erembeke: e-r̃em-be′-kay
>The custom through which a woman adopts a min-
>min

eringtingtongan: e-ring′-ting-toŋ′-an
>A type of feast which may serve as the final feast in
>honor of a deceased person

eruavalo: e-r̃u-a′-va-lo
>To mark someone of one's own moiety to contribute
>a pig at the final death feast

erumu: e-r̃u′mu
>A small payment made at a death feast which is said
>"to throw out food" received from the deceased dur-
>ing his or her lifetime

erunda: e′-r̃un-da
>Nonhuman, localized spirit, usually embodied in an
>animal, fish, snake, or object of the landscape and
>associated with a particular ebibinet

erus: e-r̃us′
>Breast, breast milk

eruwan: e-r̃u-wan′
>A couple's firstborn child

soson: so-son′
>The custom by which a person may claim a piece of
>his/her ewenteburubun's ebibinet's land at ewente-
>burubun's ekarambis death feast

eu (plural: embau): e-u′ (e^m-bau′)
>The spirit of a person who died a violent death, from
>sorcery, murder, accident, or other unnatural causes

euga: e-u′-ga
>A large final death feast

euli: e-u′-li
>The most elaborate ceremonial complex that could
>be executed as a clan's final death feast. Defunct
>since the early 1900s, the euli involved numerous
>feasts and the purchase and carving of one or more
>named wooden figures

-vasik: -va-sik′
>To procreate

evene: e-ven-e′
>Female, girl, woman

ewakandu: e-wa'-kan-du
> Dogs' teeth necklace used in exchanges

ewawagasi: e-wa-wa-ga'-si
> The cross-moiety exchange of edibles, sugarcane, coconuts, betel nuts, and peppers for money at a death feast

ewentus: e-wen'-tus
> Matrilineal, exogamous subclan or sub-subclan

Bibliography

Bateson, Gregory
1958   *Naven.* 2d ed. Stanford: Stanford University Press.

Chinnery, E. W. Pearson
1929   *Studies of the native population of the east coast of
              New Ireland.* Territory of New Guinea Anthropologi-
              cal Report no. 6. Canberra: H. J. Green, Govt.
              Printer.

Clay, R. Berle
1969   "The persistence of traditional settlement pattern:
              An example from Central New Ireland." *Oceania*
              43 (1):40–53.
1974   "Archaeological reconnaissance in Central New Ire-
              land." *Archaeology and Physical Anthropology in
              Oceania* 9 (1):1–17.

Errington, Frederick
1974*a*   "Indigenous ideas of order, time, and transition in a
              New Guinea cargo movement." *American Ethnologist*
              1 (2):255–68.
1974*b*   *Karavar: Masks and power in a Melanesian ritual.*
              Symbol, Myth, and Ritual Series. Ithaca: Cornell
              University Press.

Lewis, Phillip H.
1969   *The social context of art in Northern New Ireland.*
              Anthropological Series, vol. 58. Chicago: Field Mu-
              seum of Natural History.
1973   "Changing Memorial Ceremonial in Northern New
              Ireland." *Journal of the Polynesian Society* 82 (2):
              141–53.

Lithgow, David, and Claasen, Orev
1968   *Languages of the New Ireland District.* Ukarumpa,

Eastern Highlands District, Papua New Guinea: Summer Institute of Linguistics.

Mead, Margaret
1968   *The Mountain Arapesh.* Vol. 1. *The record of Unabelin with Rorschach analyses.* Garden City, New York: Natural History Press.

1970   *The Mountain Arapesh.* Vol. 2. *Arts and supernaturalism.* Garden City, New York: Natural History Press.

1971   *The Mountain Arapesh.* Vol. 3. *Stream of events in Alitoa.* Garden City, New York: Natural History Press.

Munn, Nancy D.
1973   *Walbiri iconography: Graphic representation and cultural symbolism in a central Australian society.* Symbol, Myth, and Ritual Series. Ithaca: Cornell University Press.

Powdermaker, Hortense
1931*a*   "Report on fieldwork in New Ireland." *Oceania* 1:357.
1931*b*   "Mortuary rites in New Ireland." *Oceania* 2:26–43.
1931*c*   "Vital statistics in New Ireland." *Human Biology* 3:351–75.

1932   "Feasts in New Ireland: The social functions of eating." *American Anthropologist* 34:236–47.
1933   *Life in Lesu: The study of a Melanesian society in New Ireland.* London: Williams and Norgate.
1966   *Stranger and friend.* New York: Norton.

Radcliffe-Brown, A. R.
1952   *Structure and function in primitive society.* New York: Free Press.

Schneider, David M.
1968   *American kinship: A cultural account.* Englewood Cliffs, N.J.: Prentice-Hall.

1972   "What is kinship all about?" In *Kinship studies in the Morgan Centennial Year,* ed. Priscilla Reining, pp. 32–63. Washington, D.C.: Anthropological Society of Washington.

Scragg, R. F. R.
1957   *Depopulation in New Ireland: A study of demography and fertility.* Territory of Papua and New Guinea Health Monograph.
1968   "Population change over twenty years in four rural New Guinea communities." Unpublished manuscript.

Wagner, Roy
1972   *Habu: The innovation of meaning in Daribi religion.* Chicago: University of Chicago Press.
1975   *The invention of culture.* Englewood Cliffs, N.J.: Prentice-Hall.

Index